MznLnx

Missing Links Exam Preps

Exam Prep for

Introductory Algebra for College Students

Blitzer, 1st Edition

The MznLnx Exam Prep is your link from the texbook and lecture to your exams.
The MznLnx Exam Preps are unauthorized and comprehensive reviews of your textbooks.

All material provided by MznLnx and Rico Publications (c) 2010
Textbook publishers and textbook authors do not particpate in or contribute to these reviews.

MznLnx

Rico Publications

Exam Prep for Introductory Algebra for College Students
1st Edition
Blitzer

Publisher: Raymond Houge
Assistant Editor: Michael Rouger
Text and Cover Designer: Lisa Buckner
Marketing Manager: Sara Swagger
Project Manager, Editorial Production: Jerry Emerson
Art Director: Vernon Lowerui

Product Manager: Dave Mason
Editorial Assitant: Rachel Guzmanji
Pedagogy: Debra Long
Cover Image: Jim Reed/Getty Images
Text and Cover Printer: City Printing, Inc.
Compositor: Media Mix, Inc.

(c) 2010 Rico Publications
ALL RIGHTS RESERVED. No part of this work covered by the copyright may be reproduced or used in any form or by an means--graphic, electronic, or mechanical, including photocopying, recording, taping, Web distribution, information storage, and retrieval systems, or in any other manner--without the written permission of the publisher.

Printed in the United States
ISBN:

For more information about our products, contact us at:
Dave.Mason@RicoPublications.com

For permission to use material from this text or product, submit a request online to:
Dave.Mason@RicoPublications.com

Contents

CHAPTER 1
The Real Number System — 1

CHAPTER 2
Linear Equations and Inequalities in One Variable — 19

CHAPTER 3
Problem Solving — 31

CHAPTER 4
Linear Equations and inequalities in Two Variables — 43

CHAPTER 5
Systems of Linear Equations and Inequalities — 55

CHAPTER 6
Exponents and Polynomials — 65

CHAPTER 7
Factoring Polynomials — 77

CHAPTER 8
Rational Expressions — 86

CHAPTER 9
Roots and Radicals — 98

CHAPTER 10
Quadratic Equations and Functions — 110

ANSWER KEY — 112

TO THE STUDENT

COMPREHENSIVE

The *MznLnx* Exam Prep series is designed to help you pass your exams. Editors at MznLnx review your textbooks and then prepare these practice exams to help you master the textbook material. Unlike study guides, workbooks, and practice tests provided by the texbook publisher and textbook authors, *MznLnx* gives you **all** of the material in each chapter in exam form, not just samples, so you can be sure to nail your exam.

MECHANICAL

The MznLnx Exam Prep series creates exams that will help you learn the subject matter as well as test you on your understanding. Each question is designed to help you master the concept. Just working through the exams, you gain an understanding of the subject--its a simple mechanical process that produces success.

INTEGRATED STUDY GUIDE AND REVIEW

MznLnx is not just a set of exams designed to test you, its also a comprehensive review of the subject content. Each exam question is also a review of the concept, making sure that you will get the answer correct without having to go to other sources of material. You learn as you go! Its the easiest way to pass an exam.

HUMOR

Studying can be tedious and dry. MznLnx's instructional design includes moderate humor within the exam questions on occassion, to break the tedium and revitalize the brain

Chapter 1. The Real Number System 1

1. A _____ is the part of a fraction that tells how many equal parts make up a whole, and which is used in the name of the fraction: "halves", "thirds", "fourths" or "quarters", "fifths" and so on.
   a. Concept
   b. Denominator0
   c. Undefined
   d. Undefined

2. In geometry, the _____ of an object is a point in some sense in the middle of the object.
   a. Thing
   b. Center0
   c. Undefined
   d. Undefined

3. The _____, the average in everyday English, which is also called the arithmetic _____ (and is distinguished from the geometric _____ or harmonic _____). The average is also called the sample _____. The expected value of a random variable, which is also called the population _____.
   a. Thing
   b. Mean0
   c. Undefined
   d. Undefined

4. A _____ is a numeral used to indicate a count. The most common use of the word today is to name the part of a fraction that tells the number or count of equal parts.
   a. Numerator0
   b. Thing
   c. Undefined
   d. Undefined

5. The _____ (symbol _____) and the millibar (symbol mbar, also mb) are units of pressure.
   a. Bar0
   b. Thing
   c. Undefined
   d. Undefined

6. In mathematics, _____ is an elementary arithmetic operation. When one of the numbers is a whole number, _____ is the repeated sum of the other number.
   a. Thing
   b. Multiplication0
   c. Undefined
   d. Undefined

7. In mathematics, a _____ is the result of multiplying, or an expression that identifies factors to be multiplied.
   a. Thing
   b. Product0
   c. Undefined
   d. Undefined

8. In mathematics, _____ geometry was the traditional name for the geometry of three-dimensional Euclidean space — for practical purposes the kind of space we live in.
   a. Solid0
   b. Thing
   c. Undefined
   d. Undefined

9. _____ is a branch of mathematics concerning the study of structure, relation and quantity.
   a. Concept
   b. Algebra0
   c. Undefined
   d. Undefined

10. Equivalence is the condition of being _____ or essentially equal.
    a. Equivalent0
    b. Thing
    c. Undefined
    d. Undefined

11. In geometry, a _____ is defined as a quadrilateral where all four of its angles are right angles.

a. Thing
b. Rectangle0
c. Undefined
d. Undefined

12. In mathematics, _____ expressions is used to reduce the expression into the lowest possible term.
a. Thing
b. Simplifying0
c. Undefined
d. Undefined

13. In mathematics, the _____ divisor of two non-zero integers, is the largest positive integer that divides both numbers without remainder.
a. Thing
b. Greatest common0
c. Undefined
d. Undefined

14. In Math the greates common divisor sometimes known as the _____ of two non- zero integers.
a. Greatest common factor0
b. Thing
c. Undefined
d. Undefined

15. _____ is the largest positive integer that divides both numbers without remainder.
a. Thing
b. Common Factor0
c. Undefined
d. Undefined

16. A _____ is a negotiable instrument instructing a financial institution to pay a specific amount of a specific currency from a specific demand account held in the maker/depositor's name with that institution. Both the maker and payee may be natural persons or legal entities.
a. Check0
b. Thing
c. Undefined
d. Undefined

17. In mathematics, a _____ is the end result of a division problem. It can also be expressed as the number of times the divisor divides into the dividend.
a. Thing
b. Quotient0
c. Undefined
d. Undefined

18. _____ the expected value of a random variable displays the average or central value of the variable. It is a summary value of the distribution of the variable.
a. Thing
b. Determining0
c. Undefined
d. Undefined

19. In mathematics, a _____ of an integer n, also called a factor of n, is an integer which evenly divides n without leaving a remainder.
a. Thing
b. Divisor0
c. Undefined
d. Undefined

20. A _____ is the result of the addition of a set of numbers. The numbers may be natural numbers, complex numbers, matrices, or still more complicated objects. An infinite _____ is a subtle procedure known as a series.
a. Thing
b. Sum0
c. Undefined
d. Undefined

Chapter 1. The Real Number System

21. _____ forms part of thinking. Considered the most complex of all intellectual functions, _____ has been defined as higher-order cognitive process that requires the modulation and control of more routine or fundamental skills.
    a. Thing
    b. Problem solving0
    c. Undefined
    d. Undefined

22. In mathematics, a _____ function in the sense of algebraic geometry is an everywhere-defined, polynomial function on an algebraic variety V with values in the field K over which V is defined.
    a. Regular0
    b. Thing
    c. Undefined
    d. Undefined

23. A _____ is a special kind of ratio, indicating a relationship between two measurements with different units, such as miles to gallons or cents to pounds.
    a. Thing
    b. Rate0
    c. Undefined
    d. Undefined

24. _____ is the amount of time someone works beyond normal working hours.
    a. Compensatory time0
    b. Thing
    c. Undefined
    d. Undefined

25. A frame of _____ is a particular perspective from which the universe is observed.
    a. Reference0
    b. Thing
    c. Undefined
    d. Undefined

26. A _____ is a function that assigns a number to subsets of a given set.
    a. Measure0
    b. Thing
    c. Undefined
    d. Undefined

27. In _____ algebra, a *-ring is an associative ring with an antilinear, antiautomorphism * : A ¨ A which is an involution.
    a. Thing
    b. Star0
    c. Undefined
    d. Undefined

28. In geographic information systems, a _____ comprises an entity with a geographic location, typically determined by points, arcs, or polygons. Carriageways and cadastres exemplify _____ data.
    a. Feature0
    b. Thing
    c. Undefined
    d. Undefined

29. A _____ is a rectangle whose side lengths are in the golden ratio, 1:, that is, approximately 1:1.618.
    a. Thing
    b. Golden rectangle0
    c. Undefined
    d. Undefined

30. A _____ is a quantity that denotes the proportional amount or magnitude of one quantity relative to another.
    a. Thing
    b. Ratio0
    c. Undefined
    d. Undefined

31. In mathematics, a _____ may be described informally as a number that can be given by an infinite decimal representation.
   a. Real number0
   b. Thing
   c. Undefined
   d. Undefined

32. In mathematics, an _____ number is any real number that is not a rational number- that is, it is a number which cannot be expressed as a fraction m/n, where m and n are integers.
   a. Irrational0
   b. Thing
   c. Undefined
   d. Undefined

33. In mathematics, an _____ is any real number that is not a rational number ¡ª that is, it is a number which cannot be expressed as m/n, where m and n are integers.
   a. Thing
   b. Irrational number0
   c. Undefined
   d. Undefined

34. In mathematics, a _____ can mean either an element of the set {1, 2, 3, ...} (i.e the positive integers or the counting numbers) or an element of the set {0, 1, 2, 3, ...} (i.e. the non-negative integers).
   a. Thing
   b. Natural number0
   c. Undefined
   d. Undefined

35. In mathematics, a _____ can mean either an element of the set {1, 2, 3, ...} (i.e the positive integers) or an element of the set {0, 1, 2, 3, ...} (i.e. the non-negative integers).
   a. Whole number0
   b. Concept
   c. Undefined
   d. Undefined

36. An _____ or member of a set is an object that when collected together make up the set.
   a. Thing
   b. Element0
   c. Undefined
   d. Undefined

37. In mathematics, the _____ , or members of a set or more generally a class are all those objects which when collected together make up the set or class.
   a. Elements0
   b. Thing
   c. Undefined
   d. Undefined

38. _____ is the mathematical action of repeatedly adding or subtracting one, usually to find out how many objects there are or to set aside a desired number of objects.
   a. Counting0
   b. Thing
   c. Undefined
   d. Undefined

39. A _____ is a one-dimensional picture in which the integers are shown as specially-marked points evenly spaced on a line.
   a. Thing
   b. Number line0
   c. Undefined
   d. Undefined

Chapter 1. The Real Number System

40. The _____ are the only integral domain whose positive elements are well-ordered, and in which order is preserved by addition. Like the natural numbers, the _____ form a countably infinite set. The set of all _____ is usually denoted in mathematics by a boldface Z .
   a. Thing
   b. Integers0
   c. Undefined
   d. Undefined

41. A _____ is a number that is less than zero.
   a. Negative number0
   b. Thing
   c. Undefined
   d. Undefined

42. In mathematics, a _____ number is a number which can be expressed as a ratio of two integers. Non-integer _____ numbers (commonly called fractions) are usually written as the vulgar fraction a / b, where b is not zero.
   a. Rational0
   b. Thing
   c. Undefined
   d. Undefined

43. A _____ decimal is a number whose decimal representation eventually becomes periodic (i.e. the same number sequence _____ indefinitely).
   a. Repeating0
   b. Thing
   c. Undefined
   d. Undefined

44. In mathematics, _____ are any real number that is not a rational number ¡ª that is, it is a number which cannot be expressed as m/n, where m and n are integers.
   a. Thing
   b. Irrational numbers0
   c. Undefined
   d. Undefined

45. In Euclidean geometry, a _____ is the set of all points in a plane at a fixed distance, called the radius, from a given point, the center.
   a. Thing
   b. Circle0
   c. Undefined
   d. Undefined

46. The _____ is the distance around a closed curve. _____ is a kind of perimeter.
   a. Thing
   b. Circumference0
   c. Undefined
   d. Undefined

47. In geometry, a _____ (Greek words diairo = divide and metro = measure) of a circle is any straight line segment that passes through the centre and whose endpoints are on the circular boundary, or, in more modern usage, the length of such a line segment. When using the word in the more modern sense, one speaks of the _____ rather than a _____, because all diameters of a circle have the same length. This length is twice the radius. The _____ of a circle is also the longest chord that the circle has.
   a. Diameter0
   b. Thing
   c. Undefined
   d. Undefined

48. _____ are objects, characters, or other concrete representations of ideas, concepts, or other abstractions.
   a. Thing
   b. Symbols0
   c. Undefined
   d. Undefined

Chapter 1. The Real Number System

49. Recurring or _____ are numbers which when expressed as decimals have a set of "final" digits which repeat an infinite number of times.
   a. Repeating decimals0
   b. Thing
   c. Undefined
   d. Undefined

50. A _____ decimal is a decimal fraction which ends after a definite number of digits.
   a. Terminating0
   b. Thing
   c. Undefined
   d. Undefined

51. In mathematics, an _____ is a statement about the relative size or order of two objects.
   a. Inequality0
   b. Thing
   c. Undefined
   d. Undefined

52. In mathematics, an inequality is a statement about the relative size or order of two objects. For example 14 > 10, or 14 is _____ 10.
   a. Thing
   b. Greater than0
   c. Undefined
   d. Undefined

53. In common philosophical language, a proposition or _____, is the content of an assertion, that is, it is true-or-false and defined by the meaning of a particular piece of language.
   a. Concept
   b. Statement0
   c. Undefined
   d. Undefined

54. _____ are the basic objects of study in graph theory. Informally speaking, a graph is a set of objects called points, nodes, or vertices connected by links called lines or edges.
   a. Graphs0
   b. Thing
   c. Undefined
   d. Undefined

55. Mathematical _____ is used to represent ideas.
   a. Notation0
   b. Thing
   c. Undefined
   d. Undefined

56. _____ is the writing of numbers in the base-ten numeral system, which uses various symbols called digits for ten distinct values 0, 1, 2, 3, 4, 5, 6, 7, 8 and 9 to represent numbers
   a. Decimal notation0
   b. Thing
   c. Undefined
   d. Undefined

57. In mathematics, the _____ (or modulus) of a real number is its numerical value without regard to its sign.
   a. Absolute value0
   b. Thing
   c. Undefined
   d. Undefined

58. The _____ of measurement are a globally standardized and modernized form of the metric system.
   a. Units0
   b. Thing
   c. Undefined
   d. Undefined

Chapter 1. The Real Number System

59. _____ is a physical property of a system that underlies the common notions of hot and cold; something that is hotter has the greater _____.
   a. Thing
   b. Temperature0
   c. Undefined
   d. Undefined

60. In combinatorial mathematics, a _____ is an un-ordered collection of unique elements.
   a. Combination0
   b. Concept
   c. Undefined
   d. Undefined

61. _____ is a temperature scale named after the German physicist Daniel Gabriel _____ , who proposed it in 1724.
   a. Thing
   b. Fahrenheit0
   c. Undefined
   d. Undefined

62. A _____ is a unit of length, usually used to measure distance, in a number of different systems, including Imperial units, United States customary units and Norwegian/Swedish mil. Its size can vary from system to system, but in each is between 1 and 10 kilometers. In contemporary English contexts _____ refers to either:
   a. Thing
   b. Mile0
   c. Undefined
   d. Undefined

63. _____ is a unit of speed, expressing the number of international miles covered per hour.
   a. Thing
   b. Miles per hour0
   c. Undefined
   d. Undefined

64. In mathematical logic, a Gödel numbering (or Gödel _____) is a function that assigns to each symbol and well-formed formula of some formal language a unique natural number called its Gödel number.
   a. Thing
   b. Code0
   c. Undefined
   d. Undefined

65. An _____ is a collection of two not necessarily distinct objects, one of which is distinguished as the first coordinate and the other as the second coordinate.
   a. Thing
   b. Ordered pair0
   c. Undefined
   d. Undefined

66. In mathematics, the conjugate _____ or adjoint matrix of an m-by-n matrix A with complex entries is the n-by-m matrix A* obtained from A by taking the transpose and then taking the complex conjugate of each entry.
   a. Thing
   b. Pairs0
   c. Undefined
   d. Undefined

67. _____ is the symbold used to indicate the nth root of a number
   a. Thing
   b. Radical0
   c. Undefined
   d. Undefined

68. _____ was an Italian physicist, mathematician, astronomer, and philosopher who is closely associated with the scientific revolution.

a. Person
b. Galileo Galilei0
c. Undefined
d. Undefined

69. _____ is the chance that something is likely to happen or be the case.
   a. Thing
   b. Probability0
   c. Undefined
   d. Undefined

70. Blaise _____ was a French mathematician, physicist, and religious philosopher.
   a. Pascal0
   b. Person
   c. Undefined
   d. Undefined

71. _____ was a highly influential French philosopher, mathematician, scientist, and writer. Dubbed the "Founder of Modern Philosophy", and the "Father of Modern Mathematics". His theories provided the basis for the calculus of Newton and Leibniz, by applying infinitesimal calculus to the tangent line problem, thus permitting the evolution of that branch of modern mathematics
   a. Descartes0
   b. Person
   c. Undefined
   d. Undefined

72. An _____ is when two lines intersect somewhere on a plane creating a right angle at intersection
   a. Thing
   b. Axes0
   c. Undefined
   d. Undefined

73. In mathematics, the _____ of a coordinate system is the point where the axes of the system intersect.
   a. Thing
   b. Origin0
   c. Undefined
   d. Undefined

74. In mathematics, the _____ of two sets A and B is the set that contains all elements of A that also belong to B (or equivalently, all elements of B that also belong to A), but no other elements.
   a. Thing
   b. Intersection0
   c. Undefined
   d. Undefined

75. A _____ consists of one quarter of the coordinate plane.
   a. Quadrant0
   b. Thing
   c. Undefined
   d. Undefined

76. In mathematics, a _____ is a two-dimensional manifold or surface that is perfectly flat.
   a. Plane0
   b. Thing
   c. Undefined
   d. Undefined

77. A _____ is a set of numbers that designate location in a given reference system, such as x,y in a planar _____ system or an x,y,z in a three-dimensional _____ system.
   a. Coordinate0
   b. Thing
   c. Undefined
   d. Undefined

78. In mathematics and its applications, a _____ is a system for assigning an n-tuple of numbers or scalars to each point in an n-dimensional space.

Chapter 1. The Real Number System

a. Coordinate system0
b. Concept
c. Undefined
d. Undefined

79. A _____ ratio, also called, Lift-to-drag ratio, _____ number, or finesse, is an aviation term that refers to the distance an aircraft will move forward for any given amount of lost altitude .
a. Glide0
b. Thing
c. Undefined
d. Undefined

80. An _____ is a straight line around which a geometric figure can be rotated.
a. Axis0
b. Thing
c. Undefined
d. Undefined

81. In astronomy, geography, geometry and related sciences and contexts, a plane is said to be _____ at a given point if it is locally perpendicular to the gradient of the gravity field, i.e., with the direction of the gravitational force at that point.
a. Thing
b. Horizontal0
c. Undefined
d. Undefined

82. _____ is a kind of property which exists as magnitude or multitude. It is among the basic classes of things along with quality, substance, change, and relation.
a. Amount0
b. Thing
c. Undefined
d. Undefined

83. In geometry, a line _____ is a part of a line that is bounded by two end points, and contains every point on the line between its end points.
a. Concept
b. Segment0
c. Undefined
d. Undefined

84. A _____ is a part of a line that is bounded by two end points, and contains every point on the line between its end points.
a. Thing
b. Line segment0
c. Undefined
d. Undefined

85. In mathematics, an _____, mean, or central tendency of a data set refers to a measure of the "middle" or "expected" value of the data set.
a. Average0
b. Concept
c. Undefined
d. Undefined

86. In business, particularly accounting, a _____ is the time intervals that the accounts, statement, payments, or other calculations cover.
a. Thing
b. Period0
c. Undefined
d. Undefined

87. In finance, a _____ is collateral that the holder of a position in securities, options, or futures contracts has to deposit to cover the credit risk of his counterparty.

a. Margin0
b. Thing
c. Undefined
d. Undefined

88. _____ (Groups, Algorithms and Programming) is a computer algebra system for computational discrete algebra with particular emphasis on, but not restricted to, computational group theory.
   a. Gap0
   b. Thing
   c. Undefined
   d. Undefined

89. In sociology and biology a _____ is the collection of people or organisms of a particular species living in a given geographic area or space, usually measured by a census.
   a. Thing
   b. Population0
   c. Undefined
   d. Undefined

90. A circular _____ or circle _____ also known as a pie piece is the portion of a circle enclosed by two radii and an arc.
   a. Thing
   b. Sector0
   c. Undefined
   d. Undefined

91. The decimal separator is a symbol used to mark the boundary between the integral and the fractional parts of a decimal numeral. Terms implying the symbol used are _____ and decimal comma.
   a. Concept
   b. Decimal point0
   c. Undefined
   d. Undefined

92. _____ is a way of expressing a number as a fraction of 100 per cent meaning "per hundred".
   a. Thing
   b. Percent0
   c. Undefined
   d. Undefined

93. _____ is the transport of people on a trip/journey or the process or time involved in a person or object moving from one location to another.
   a. Thing
   b. Travel0
   c. Undefined
   d. Undefined

94. _____ is a statistical measure of the average length of survival of a living thing.
   a. Life expectancy0
   b. Thing
   c. Undefined
   d. Undefined

95. A bar chart, also known as a _____, is a chart with rectangular bars of lengths usually proportional to the magnitudes or frequencies of what they represent.
   a. Thing
   b. Bar graph0
   c. Undefined
   d. Undefined

96. _____ are activities that are governed by a set of rules or customs and often engaged in competitively.
   a. Thing
   b. Sports0
   c. Undefined
   d. Undefined

Chapter 1. The Real Number System 11

97. In mathematics, an _____ on a real vector space is a choice of which ordered bases are "positively" oriented, or right-handed, and which are "negatively" oriented, or left-handed.
   a. Orientation0
   b. Thing
   c. Undefined
   d. Undefined

98. _____ are procedures that allow people to exchange information by one of several methods.
   a. Communications0
   b. Thing
   c. Undefined
   d. Undefined

99. In mathematics and logic, a _____ proof is a way of showing the truth or falsehood of a given statement by a straightforward combination of established facts, usually existing lemmas and theorems, without making any further assumptions.
   a. Thing
   b. Direct0
   c. Undefined
   d. Undefined

100. A _____ is a symbolic representation denoting a quantity or expression. It often represents an "unknown" quantity that has the potential to change.
   a. Thing
   b. Variable0
   c. Undefined
   d. Undefined

101. An _____ is a combination of numbers, operators, grouping symbols and/or free variables and bound variables arranged in a meaningful way which can be evaluated..
   a. Thing
   b. Expression0
   c. Undefined
   d. Undefined

102. In mathematics, a _____ of a complex-valued function f is a member x of the domain of f such that f(x) vanishes at x, that is, x : f (x) = 0.
   a. Thing
   b. Root0
   c. Undefined
   d. Undefined

103. _____ has many meanings, most of which simply .
   a. Power0
   b. Thing
   c. Undefined
   d. Undefined

104. In mathematics, a _____ is a constant multiplicative factor of a certain object. The object can be such things as a variable, a vector, a function, etc. For example, the _____ of $9x^2$ is 9.
   a. Thing
   b. Coefficient0
   c. Undefined
   d. Undefined

105. In mathematics and the mathematical sciences, a _____ is a fixed, but possibly unspecified, value. This is in contrast to a variable, which is not fixed.
   a. Constant0
   b. Thing
   c. Undefined
   d. Undefined

106. _____ is a fixed, but possibly unspecified, value. This is in contrast to a variable, which is not fixed.

a. Thing
b. Constant term0
c. Undefined
d. Undefined

107. In mathematics, factorization (British English: factorisation) or factoring is the decomposition of an object (for example, a number, a polynomial, or a matrix) into a product of other objects, or _____, which when multiplied together give the original.
a. Factors0
b. Thing
c. Undefined
d. Undefined

108. A _____ is 360° or 2δ radians.
a. Turn0
b. Thing
c. Undefined
d. Undefined

109. The _____ is a property of multiplication or addition where the product or sum remains the same, regardless of whether or not the order of the addends or factors are changed.
a. Commutative property0
b. Thing
c. Undefined
d. Undefined

110. In abstract algebra, _____ consists of sets with binary operations that satisfy certain axioms.
a. Thing
b. Grouping0
c. Undefined
d. Undefined

111. In mathematics, _____ is a property that a binary operation can have. Within an expression containing two or more of the same associative operators in a row, the order of operations does not matter as long as the sequence of the operands is not changed.
a. Thing
b. Associativity0
c. Undefined
d. Undefined

112. _____, either of the curved-bracket punctuation marks that together make a set of _____
a. Parentheses0
b. Thing
c. Undefined
d. Undefined

113. In mathematics, and in particular in abstract algebra, the _____ is a property of binary operations that generalises the distributive law from elementary algebra.
a. Distributive property0
b. Thing
c. Undefined
d. Undefined

114. A _____ is a consumption tax charged at the point of purchase for certain goods and services.
a. Sales tax0
b. Thing
c. Undefined
d. Undefined

115. In linear algebra, the _____ of a matrix A is another matrix AT
a. Transpose0
b. Thing
c. Undefined
d. Undefined

Chapter 1. The Real Number System

116. Fixed costs are expenses whose total does not change in proportion to the activity of a business. Unit fixed costs decline with volume following a retangular hyperbola as the volume of production. Variable costs by contrast change in relation to the activity of a business such as sales or production volume. Along with variable costs, fixed costs make up one of the two components of total cost. In the most simple production function total cost is equal to fixed costs plus variable costs. In accounting terminology, fixed costs will broadly include all costs which are not included in cost of goods sold, and variable costs are those captured in costs of goods sold. The implicit assumption required to make the equivalence between the accounting and economics terminology is that the accounting period is equal to the period in which fixed costs do not vary in relation to production. In practice, this equivalence does not always hold and depending on the period under consideration by management, some overhead expenses can be adjusted by management, and the specific allocation of each expense to each category will be decided under cost accounting. In business planning and management accounting, usage of the terms fixed costs, variable costs and others will often differ from usage in economics, and may depend on the intended use. For example, costs may be segregated into per unit costs fixed costs per period, and variable costs as a proportion of revenue. Capital expenditures will usually be allocated separately, and depending on the purpose, a portion may be regularly allocated to expenses as depreciation and amortization and seen as a _____ per period, or the entire amount may be considered upfront fixed costs.
- a. Thing
- b. Fixed cost0
- c. Undefined
- d. Undefined

117. _____ are expenses whose total does not change in proportion to the activity of a business, within the relevant time period or scale of production
- a. Fixed costs0
- b. Thing
- c. Undefined
- d. Undefined

118. _____, from Latin meaning "to make progress", is defined in two different ways. Pure economic _____ is the increase in wealth that an investor has from making an investment, taking into consideration all costs associated with that investment including the opportunity cost of capital.
- a. Profit0
- b. Thing
- c. Undefined
- d. Undefined

119. In mathematics, the additive inverse, or _____ of a number n is the number that, when added to n, yields zero. The additive inverse of n is denoted −n. For example, 7 is −7, because 7 + (−7) = 0, and the additive inverse of −0.3 is 0.3, because −0.3 + 0.3 = 0.
- a. Thing
- b. Opposite0
- c. Undefined
- d. Undefined

120. _____ element of an element x with respect to a binary operation * with identity element e is an element y such that x * y = y * x = e. In particular,
- a. Inverse0
- b. Thing
- c. Undefined
- d. Undefined

121. In mathematics, the _____ inverse, or opposite, of a number n is the number that, when added to n, yields zero. The _____ inverse of n is denoted −n.
- a. Additive0
- b. Thing
- c. Undefined
- d. Undefined

Chapter 1. The Real Number System

122. In mathematics, the _____ of a number n is the number that, when added to n, yields zero. The _____ of n is denoted −n. For example, 7 is −7, because 7 + (−7) = 0, and the _____ of −0.3 is 0.3, because −0.3 + 0.3 = 0.
   a. Thing
   b. Additive inverse0
   c. Undefined
   d. Undefined

123. An _____ is an equality that remains true regardless of the values of any variables that appear within it, to distinguish it from an equality which is true under more particular conditions.
   a. Thing
   b. Identity0
   c. Undefined
   d. Undefined

124. In mathematics the _____ of a set which is equipped with the operation of addition is an element which, when added to any other element x in the set, yields x.
   a. Concept
   b. Additive identity0
   c. Undefined
   d. Undefined

125. A _____ is the sum of the elements of a sequence.
   a. Thing
   b. Series0
   c. Undefined
   d. Undefined

126. The metre (or _____, see spelling differences) is a measure of length. It is the basic unit of length in the metric system and in the International System of Units (SI), used around the world for general and scientific purposes.
   a. Meter0
   b. Concept
   c. Undefined
   d. Undefined

127. In mathematics, a _____ or rhodonea curve is a sinusoid plotted in polar coordinates.
   a. Thing
   b. Rose0
   c. Undefined
   d. Undefined

128. In mathematics, there are several meanings of _____ depending on the subject.
   a. Degree0
   b. Thing
   c. Undefined
   d. Undefined

129. _____ are a measure of time.
   a. Minutes0
   b. Thing
   c. Undefined
   d. Undefined

130. In mathematics, a matrix can be thought of as each row or _____ being a vector. Hence, a space formed by row vectors or _____ vectors are said to be a row space or a _____ space.
   a. Concept
   b. Column0
   c. Undefined
   d. Undefined

131. In topology and related areas of mathematics a _____ or Moore-Smith sequence is a generalization of a sequence, intended to unify the various notions of limit and generalize them to arbitrary topological spaces.
   a. Thing
   b. Net0
   c. Undefined
   d. Undefined

132. _____ primarily refers to social welfare service concerned with social protection, or protection against socially recognized conditions, including poverty, old age, disability, unemployment, families with children and others.
   a. Social security0
   b. Thing
   c. Undefined
   d. Undefined

133. _____ usually refers to money in the form of liquid currency, such as banknotes or coins.
   a. Cash0
   b. Thing
   c. Undefined
   d. Undefined

134. A recession (i.e. _____) is traditionally defined in macroeconomics as a decline in a country's real Gross Domestic Product (GDP) for two or more successive quarters of a year (equivalently, two consecutive quarters of negative real economic growth).
   a. Thing
   b. Depression0
   c. Undefined
   d. Undefined

135. _____ is electromagnetic radiation with a wavelength that is visible to the eye (visible _____) or, in a technical or scientific context, electromagnetic radiation of any wavelength.
   a. Thing
   b. Light0
   c. Undefined
   d. Undefined

136. _____ is the application of tools and a processing medium to the transformation of raw materials into finished goods for sale.
   a. Manufacturing0
   b. Thing
   c. Undefined
   d. Undefined

137. In mathematics, the _____ inverse of a number x, denoted 1/x or x^{-1}, is the number which, when multiplied by x, yields 1. The _____ inverse of x is also called the reciprocal of x.
   a. Thing
   b. Multiplicative0
   c. Undefined
   d. Undefined

138. In mathematics, defined and _____ are used to explain whether or not expressions have meaningful, sensible, and unambiguous values.
   a. Undefined0
   b. Thing
   c. Undefined
   d. Undefined

139. The _____ integers are all the integers from zero on upwards.
   a. Thing
   b. Nonnegative0
   c. Undefined
   d. Undefined

140. _____ is a form of periodic payment from an employer to an employee, which is specified in an employment contract.
   a. Thing
   b. Gross pay0
   c. Undefined
   d. Undefined

141. A _____ is a form of periodic payment from an employer to an employee, which is specified in an employment contract.

a. Thing
b. Salary0
c. Undefined
d. Undefined

142. _____ is a mathematical operation, written a^n, involving two numbers, the base a and the exponent n.
a. Exponentiating0
b. Thing
c. Undefined
d. Undefined

143. _____ is a mathematical operation, written a^n, involving two numbers, the base a and the exponent n.
a. Thing
b. Exponentiation0
c. Undefined
d. Undefined

144. In mathematics, _____ growth occurs when the growth rate of a function is always proportional to the function's current size.
a. Thing
b. Exponential0
c. Undefined
d. Undefined

145. In arithmetic and algebra, when a number or expression is both preceded and followed by a binary operation, an _____ is required for which operation should be applied first.
a. Order of operations0
b. Thing
c. Undefined
d. Undefined

146. A _____ is an abstract model that uses mathematical language to describe the behavior of a system. Eykhoff defined a _____ as 'a representation of the essential aspects of an existing system which presents knowledge of that system in usable form'.
a. Thing
b. Mathematical model0
c. Undefined
d. Undefined

147. In mathematics, a subset of Euclidean space R^n is called _____ if it is closed and bounded.
a. Thing
b. Compact0
c. Undefined
d. Undefined

148. The population _____ is the total number of human beings alive on the planet Earth at a given time.
a. Of the world0
b. Thing
c. Undefined
d. Undefined

149. Celsius is, or relates to, the Celsius temperature scale (previously known as the centigrade scale). The degree Celsius (symbol: °C) can refer to a specific temperature on the _____ as well as serve as unit increment to indicate a temperature interval (a difference between two temperatures or an uncertainty).
a. Celsius Scale0
b. Concept
c. Undefined
d. Undefined

150. The _____ is a temperature scale named after the German physicist Daniel Gabriel Fahrenheit (1686–1736), who proposed it in 1724.
a. Fahrenheit scale0
b. Thing
c. Undefined
d. Undefined

Chapter 1. The Real Number System 17

151. _____ is, or relates to, the _____ temperature scale .
   a. Celsius0
   b. Thing
   c. Undefined
   d. Undefined

152. In Euclidean geometry, a uniform _____ is a linear transformation that enlargers or diminishes objects, and whose _____ factor is the same in all directions. This is also called homothethy.
   a. Scale0
   b. Thing
   c. Undefined
   d. Undefined

153. In Graph theory, a _____ is a digraph with weighted edges.
   a. Network0
   b. Concept
   c. Undefined
   d. Undefined

154. _____ is a synonym for information.
   a. Data0
   b. Thing
   c. Undefined
   d. Undefined

155. _____ is a set, with some particular properties and usually some additional structure, such as the operations of addition or multiplication, for instance.
   a. Thing
   b. Space0
   c. Undefined
   d. Undefined

156. The _____ of a ring R is defined to be the smallest positive integer n such that n a = 0, for all a in R.
   a. Characteristic0
   b. Thing
   c. Undefined
   d. Undefined

157. _____ is the estimation of a physical quantity such as distance, energy, temperature, or time.
   a. Thing
   b. Measurement0
   c. Undefined
   d. Undefined

158. The word _____ is used in a variety of ways in mathematics.
   a. Index0
   b. Thing
   c. Undefined
   d. Undefined

159. Mathematical _____ are the wide variety of ways to capture an abstract mathematical concept or relationship.
   a. Representations0
   b. Thing
   c. Undefined
   d. Undefined

160. In geometry, _____ lines are two lines that share one or more common points.
   a. Intersecting0
   b. Thing
   c. Undefined
   d. Undefined

161. In mathematics, the multiplicative inverse of a number x, denoted 1/x or x^{-1}, is the number which, when multiplied by x, yields 1. The multiplicative inverse of x is also called the _____ of x.

a. Reciprocal0
c. Undefined
b. Thing
d. Undefined

162. Two mathematical objects are equal if and only if they are precisely the same in every way. This defines a binary relation, _____, denoted by the sign of _____ "=" in such a way that the statement "x = y" means that x and y are equal.
   a. Thing
   b. Equality0
   c. Undefined
   d. Undefined

163. _____ is the ability to hold, receive or absorb, or a measure thereof, similar to the concept of volume.
   a. Capacity0
   b. Concept
   c. Undefined
   d. Undefined

164. The _____ of a geographic location is its height above a fixed reference point, often the mean sea level.
   a. Thing
   b. Elevation0
   c. Undefined
   d. Undefined

165. A _____ is a statement or claimt that a particular event will occur in the future in more certain terms than a forecast.
   a. Thing
   b. Prediction0
   c. Undefined
   d. Undefined

Chapter 2. Linear Equations and Inequalities in One Variable

1. Two mathematical objects are equal if and only if they are precisely the same in every way. This defines a binary relation, _____, denoted by the sign of _____ "=" in such a way that the statement "x = y" means that x and y are equal.
   a. Thing
   b. Equality0
   c. Undefined
   d. Undefined

2. _____ is a kind of property which exists as magnitude or multitude. It is among the basic classes of things along with quality, substance, change, and relation.
   a. Thing
   b. Amount0
   c. Undefined
   d. Undefined

3. A _____ is a unit of length, usually used to measure distance, in a number of different systems, including Imperial units, United States customary units and Norwegian/Swedish mil. Its size can vary from system to system, but in each is between 1 and 10 kilometers. In contemporary English contexts _____ refers to either:
   a. Thing
   b. Mile0
   c. Undefined
   d. Undefined

4. _____ is a unit of speed, expressing the number of international miles covered per hour.
   a. Thing
   b. Miles per hour0
   c. Undefined
   d. Undefined

5. _____, in economics and political economy, are the distributions or payments awarded to the various suppliers of the factors of production.
   a. Returns0
   b. Thing
   c. Undefined
   d. Undefined

6. There are two main approaches to _____ in mathematics. They are the model theory of _____ and the proof theory of _____.
   a. Thing
   b. Truth0
   c. Undefined
   d. Undefined

7. _____ is a branch of mathematics concerning the study of structure, relation and quantity.
   a. Algebra0
   b. Concept
   c. Undefined
   d. Undefined

8. In common philosophical language, a proposition or _____, is the content of an assertion, that is, it is true-or-false and defined by the meaning of a particular piece of language.
   a. Concept
   b. Statement0
   c. Undefined
   d. Undefined

9. An _____ is a combination of numbers, operators, grouping symbols and/or free variables and bound variables arranged in a meaningful way which can be evaluated..
   a. Expression0
   b. Thing
   c. Undefined
   d. Undefined

10. A _____ is a symbolic representation denoting a quantity or expression. It often represents an "unknown" quantity that has the potential to change.

a. Variable0 b. Thing
c. Undefined d. Undefined

11. The word _____ comes from the Latin word linearis, which means created by lines.
a. Linear0 b. Thing
c. Undefined d. Undefined

12. A _____ is an equation in which each term is either a constant or the product of a constant times the first power of a variable.
a. Linear equation0 b. Thing
c. Undefined d. Undefined

13. A _____ is a negotiable instrument instructing a financial institution to pay a specific amount of a specific currency from a specific demand account held in the maker/depositor's name with that institution. Both the maker and payee may be natural persons or legal entities.
a. Thing b. Check0
c. Undefined d. Undefined

14. Equivalence is the condition of being _____ or essentially equal.
a. Equivalent0 b. Thing
c. Undefined d. Undefined

15. In mathematics, a _____ may be described informally as a number that can be given by an infinite decimal representation.
a. Real number0 b. Thing
c. Undefined d. Undefined

16. A _____ is a set of possible values that a variable can take on in order to satisfy a given set of conditions, which may include equations and inequalities.
a. Solution set0 b. Thing
c. Undefined d. Undefined

17. _____ is a mathematical notation for describing a set by stating the properties that its members must satisfy.
a. Set-builder notation0 b. Thing
c. Undefined d. Undefined

18. Mathematical _____ is used to represent ideas.
a. Notation0 b. Thing
c. Undefined d. Undefined

19. In Euclidean geometry, a uniform _____ is a linear transformation that enlargers or diminishes objects, and whose _____ factor is the same in all directions. This is also called homothethy.
a. Scale0 b. Thing
c. Undefined d. Undefined

Chapter 2. Linear Equations and Inequalities in One Variable

20. In banking and accountancy, the outstanding _____ is the amount of money owned, or due, that remains in a deposit account or a loan account at a given date, after all past remittances, payments and withdrawal have been accounted for.
    a. Thing
    b. Balance0
    c. Undefined
    d. Undefined

21. A _____ is the part of a fraction that tells how many equal parts make up a whole, and which is used in the name of the fraction: "halves", "thirds", "fourths" or "quarters", "fifths" and so on.
    a. Concept
    b. Denominator0
    c. Undefined
    d. Undefined

22. _____ are a measure of time.
    a. Thing
    b. Minutes0
    c. Undefined
    d. Undefined

23. A _____ is a number that is less than zero.
    a. Negative number0
    b. Thing
    c. Undefined
    d. Undefined

24. In mathematics and the mathematical sciences, a _____ is a fixed, but possibly unspecified, value. This is in contrast to a variable, which is not fixed.
    a. Thing
    b. Constant0
    c. Undefined
    d. Undefined

25. _____ is a fixed, but possibly unspecified, value. This is in contrast to a variable, which is not fixed.
    a. Constant term0
    b. Thing
    c. Undefined
    d. Undefined

26. A _____ is a set of numbers that designate location in a given reference system, such as x,y in a planar _____ system or an x,y,z in a three-dimensional _____ system.
    a. Thing
    b. Coordinate0
    c. Undefined
    d. Undefined

27. In mathematics and its applications, a _____ is a system for assigning an n-tuple of numbers or scalars to each point in an n-dimensional space.
    a. Concept
    b. Coordinate system0
    c. Undefined
    d. Undefined

28. _____ is a synonym for information.
    a. Data0
    b. Thing
    c. Undefined
    d. Undefined

29. _____ is the level of functional and/or metabolic efficiency of an organism at both the micro level.
    a. Health0
    b. Thing
    c. Undefined
    d. Undefined

Chapter 2. Linear Equations and Inequalities in One Variable

30. _____ is a term used in marketing to indicate how much the price of a product is above the cost of producing and distributing the product.
   a. Thing
   b. Markup0
   c. Undefined
   d. Undefined

31. In mathematics, an _____, mean, or central tendency of a data set refers to a measure of the "middle" or "expected" value of the data set.
   a. Average0
   b. Concept
   c. Undefined
   d. Undefined

32. In mathematics, _____ is an elementary arithmetic operation. When one of the numbers is a whole number, _____ is the repeated sum of the other number.
   a. Thing
   b. Multiplication0
   c. Undefined
   d. Undefined

33. In geometry, the _____ of an object is a point in some sense in the middle of the object.
   a. Center0
   b. Thing
   c. Undefined
   d. Undefined

34. In mathematics, a _____ is a constant multiplicative factor of a certain object. The object can be such things as a variable, a vector, a function, etc. For example, the _____ of $9x^2$ is 9.
   a. Coefficient0
   b. Thing
   c. Undefined
   d. Undefined

35. In mathematics, the _____ inverse of a number x, denoted 1/x or x^{-1}, is the number which, when multiplied by x, yields 1. The _____ inverse of x is also called the reciprocal of x.
   a. Multiplicative0
   b. Thing
   c. Undefined
   d. Undefined

36. _____ element of an element x with respect to a binary operation * with identity element e is an element y such that x * y = y * x = e. In particular,
   a. Thing
   b. Inverse0
   c. Undefined
   d. Undefined

37. The _____, the average in everyday English, which is also called the arithmetic _____ (and is distinguished from the geometric _____ or harmonic _____). The average is also called the sample _____. The expected value of a random variable, which is also called the population _____.
   a. Thing
   b. Mean0
   c. Undefined
   d. Undefined

38. In mathematics, the additive inverse, or _____ of a number n is the number that, when added to n, yields zero. The additive inverse of n is denoted −n. For example, 7 is −7, because 7 + (−7) = 0, and the additive inverse of −0.3 is 0.3, because −0.3 + 0.3 = 0.
   a. Thing
   b. Opposite0
   c. Undefined
   d. Undefined

Chapter 2. Linear Equations and Inequalities in One Variable

39. In mathematics, the _____ inverse, or opposite, of a number n is the number that, when added to n, yields zero. The _____ inverse of n is denoted −n.
   a. Additive0
   b. Thing
   c. Undefined
   d. Undefined

40. In mathematics, the _____ of a number n is the number that, when added to n, yields zero. The _____ of n is denoted −n. For example, 7 is −7, because 7 + (−7) = 0, and the _____ of −0.3 is 0.3, because −0.3 + 0.3 = 0.
   a. Additive inverse0
   b. Thing
   c. Undefined
   d. Undefined

41. _____ is a statistical measure of the average length of survival of a living thing.
   a. Thing
   b. Life expectancy0
   c. Undefined
   d. Undefined

42. The _____ (symbol _____) and the millibar (symbol mbar, also mb) are units of pressure.
   a. Thing
   b. Bar0
   c. Undefined
   d. Undefined

43. A bar chart, also known as a _____, is a chart with rectangular bars of lengths usually proportional to the magnitudes or frequencies of what they represent.
   a. Thing
   b. Bar graph0
   c. Undefined
   d. Undefined

44. A _____ is a special kind of ratio, indicating a relationship between two measurements with different units, such as miles to gallons or cents to pounds.
   a. Rate0
   b. Thing
   c. Undefined
   d. Undefined

45. _____ or arithmetics is the oldest and most elementary branch of mathematics, used by almost everyone, for tasks ranging from simple daily counting to advanced science and business calculations.
   a. Arithmetic0
   b. Thing
   c. Undefined
   d. Undefined

46. _____, either of the curved-bracket punctuation marks that together make a set of _____
   a. Parentheses0
   b. Thing
   c. Undefined
   d. Undefined

47. In mathematics, and in particular in abstract algebra, the _____ is a property of binary operations that generalises the distributive law from elementary algebra.
   a. Thing
   b. Distributive property0
   c. Undefined
   d. Undefined

48. Regrouping is the act of putting ones into groups of 10. For example, the 1 on the far right of 131 would be denoted _____ if the digit of the number being subtracted is larger than 1, such as 131-99.

Chapter 2. Linear Equations and Inequalities in One Variable

a. By 100
b. Thing
c. Undefined
d. Undefined

49. In mathematics, a _____ of an integer n, also called a factor of n, is an integer which evenly divides n without leaving a remainder.
a. Thing
b. Divisor0
c. Undefined
d. Undefined

50. _____ is the largest positive integer that divides both numbers without remainder.
a. Common Factor0
b. Thing
c. Undefined
d. Undefined

51. In mathematics, factorization (British English: factorisation) or factoring is the decomposition of an object (for example, a number, a polynomial, or a matrix) into a product of other objects, or _____, which when multiplied together give the original.
a. Factors0
b. Thing
c. Undefined
d. Undefined

52. An _____ is an equality that remains true regardless of the values of any variables that appear within it, to distinguish it from an equality which is true under more particular conditions.
a. Thing
b. Identity0
c. Undefined
d. Undefined

53. _____ is a temperature scale named after the German physicist Daniel Gabriel _____ , who proposed it in 1724.
a. Fahrenheit0
b. Thing
c. Undefined
d. Undefined

54. In mathematics, there are several meanings of _____ depending on the subject.
a. Thing
b. Degree0
c. Undefined
d. Undefined

55. _____ is a physical property of a system that underlies the common notions of hot and cold; something that is hotter has the greater _____.
a. Thing
b. Temperature0
c. Undefined
d. Undefined

56. In plane geometry, a _____ is a polygon with four equal sides, four right angles, and parallel opposite sides. In algebra, the _____ of a number is that number multiplied by itself.
a. Square0
b. Thing
c. Undefined
d. Undefined

57. A _____ is an abstract model that uses mathematical language to describe the behavior of a system. Eykhoff defined a _____ as 'a representation of the essential aspects of an existing system which presents knowledge of that system in usable form'.

Chapter 2. Linear Equations and Inequalities in One Variable

a. Mathematical model0
b. Thing
c. Undefined
d. Undefined

58. _____ is a way of expressing a number as a fraction of 100 per cent meaning "per hundred".
   a. Percent0
   b. Thing
   c. Undefined
   d. Undefined

59. The _____ of measurement are a globally standardized and modernized form of the metric system.
   a. Units0
   b. Thing
   c. Undefined
   d. Undefined

60. In geometry, a _____ is defined as a quadrilateral where all four of its angles are right angles.
   a. Thing
   b. Rectangle0
   c. Undefined
   d. Undefined

61. A _____ is a function that assigns a number to subsets of a given set.
   a. Measure0
   b. Thing
   c. Undefined
   d. Undefined

62. In mathematics, a _____ is the result of multiplying, or an expression that identifies factors to be multiplied.
   a. Product0
   b. Thing
   c. Undefined
   d. Undefined

63. A _____ is the result of the addition of a set of numbers. The numbers may be natural numbers, complex numbers, matrices, or still more complicated objects. An infinite _____ is a subtle procedure known as a series.
   a. Thing
   b. Sum0
   c. Undefined
   d. Undefined

64. _____ is the distance around a given two-dimensional object. As a general rule, the _____ of a polygon can always be calculated by adding all the length of the sides together. So, the formula for triangles is P = a + b + c, where a, b and c stand for each side of it. For quadrilaterals the equation is P = a + b + c + d. For equilateral polygons, P = na, where n is the number of sides and a is the side length.
   a. Perimeter0
   b. Thing
   c. Undefined
   d. Undefined

65. The decimal separator is a symbol used to mark the boundary between the integral and the fractional parts of a decimal numeral. Terms implying the symbol used are _____ and decimal comma.
   a. Concept
   b. Decimal point0
   c. Undefined
   d. Undefined

66. U.S. liquid _____ is legally defined as 231 cubic inches, and is equal to 3.785411784 litres or abotu 0.13368 cubic feet. This is the most common definition of a _____. The U.S. fluid ounce is defined as 1/128 of a U.S. _____.
   a. Thing
   b. Gallon0
   c. Undefined
   d. Undefined

Chapter 2. Linear Equations and Inequalities in One Variable

67. _____ is, or relates to, the _____ temperature scale .
   a. Thing
   b. Celsius0
   c. Undefined
   d. Undefined

68. In Euclidean geometry, a _____ is the set of all points in a plane at a fixed distance, called the radius, from a given point, the center.
   a. Circle0
   b. Thing
   c. Undefined
   d. Undefined

69. _____ are the basic objects of study in graph theory. Informally speaking, a graph is a set of objects called points, nodes, or vertices connected by links called lines or edges.
   a. Thing
   b. Graphs0
   c. Undefined
   d. Undefined

70. In mathematics, a _____ is the end result of a division problem. It can also be expressed as the number of times the divisor divides into the dividend.
   a. Thing
   b. Quotient0
   c. Undefined
   d. Undefined

71. An _____ is a score derived from one of several different standardized tests attempting to measure intelligence.
   a. Intelligence Quotient0
   b. Thing
   c. Undefined
   d. Undefined

72. _____ of an object is its speed in a particular direction.
   a. Velocity0
   b. Thing
   c. Undefined
   d. Undefined

73. _____ over a given field is a polynomial with coefficients in that field.
   a. Thing
   b. Algebraic equation0
   c. Undefined
   d. Undefined

74. In Euclidean geometry, a _____ is moving every point a constant distance in a specified direction.
   a. Concept
   b. Translation0
   c. Undefined
   d. Undefined

75. In mathematics, the multiplicative inverse of a number x, denoted 1/x or x^{-1}, is the number which, when multiplied by x, yields 1. The multiplicative inverse of x is also called the _____ of x.
   a. Thing
   b. Reciprocal0
   c. Undefined
   d. Undefined

76. The plus and _____ signs are mathematical symbols used to represent the notions of positive and negative as well as the operations of addition and subtraction.
   a. Minus0
   b. Thing
   c. Undefined
   d. Undefined

Chapter 2. Linear Equations and Inequalities in One Variable

77. In sociology and biology a _____ is the collection of people or organisms of a particular species living in a given geographic area or space, usually measured by a census.
   a. Population0
   b. Thing
   c. Undefined
   d. Undefined

78. _____ forms part of thinking. Considered the most complex of all intellectual functions, _____ has been defined as higher-order cognitive process that requires the modulation and control of more routine or fundamental skills.
   a. Problem solving0
   b. Thing
   c. Undefined
   d. Undefined

79. Multiple Signal Classification, also known as _____, is an algorithm used for frequency estimation and emitter location.
   a. Music0
   b. Thing
   c. Undefined
   d. Undefined

80. The _____ are the only integral domain whose positive elements are well-ordered, and in which order is preserved by addition. Like the natural numbers, the _____ form a countably infinite set. The set of all _____ is usually denoted in mathematics by a boldface Z .
   a. Integers0
   b. Thing
   c. Undefined
   d. Undefined

81. _____ means in succession or back-to-back
   a. Thing
   b. Consecutive0
   c. Undefined
   d. Undefined

82. _____ is the transport of people on a trip/journey or the process or time involved in a person or object moving from one location to another.
   a. Thing
   b. Travel0
   c. Undefined
   d. Undefined

83. A _____ is 360° or 2∂ radians.
   a. Turn0
   b. Thing
   c. Undefined
   d. Undefined

84. The metre (or _____, see spelling differences) is a measure of length. It is the basic unit of length in the metric system and in the International System of Units (SI), used around the world for general and scientific purposes.
   a. Concept
   b. Meter0
   c. Undefined
   d. Undefined

85. In mathematics, _____ refers to the rewriting of an expression into a simpler form.
   a. Reduction0
   b. Thing
   c. Undefined
   d. Undefined

86. Transport or _____ is the movement of people and goods from one place to another.

a. Transportation0 b. Thing
c. Undefined d. Undefined

87. _____ is a state located in the southern and southwestern regions of the United States of America.
    a. Texas0 b. Thing
    c. Undefined d. Undefined

88. A _____ is a consumption tax charged at the point of purchase for certain goods and services.
    a. Sales tax0 b. Thing
    c. Undefined d. Undefined

89. A _____ is the part of the dividend that is left over when the dividend is not evenly divisible by the divisor.
    a. Remainder0 b. Thing
    c. Undefined d. Undefined

90. In geographic information systems, a _____ comprises an entity with a geographic location, typically determined by points, arcs, or polygons. Carriageways and cadastres exemplify _____ data.
    a. Feature0 b. Thing
    c. Undefined d. Undefined

91. In mathematics, an _____ is a statement about the relative size or order of two objects.
    a. Thing b. Inequality0
    c. Undefined d. Undefined

92. The _____ is a property of multiplication or addition where the product or sum remains the same, regardless of whether or not the order of the addends or factors are changed.
    a. Thing b. Commutative property0
    c. Undefined d. Undefined

93. A _____ is a one-dimensional picture in which the integers are shown as specially-marked points evenly spaced on a line.
    a. Thing b. Number line0
    c. Undefined d. Undefined

94. In geometry, an _____ is a point at which a line segment or ray terminates.
    a. Endpoint0 b. Thing
    c. Undefined d. Undefined

95. In mathematics, an inequality is a statement about the relative size or order of two objects. For example 14 > 10, or 14 is _____ 10.
    a. Thing b. Greater than0
    c. Undefined d. Undefined

96. An _____ or member of a set is an object that when collected together make up the set.

Chapter 2. Linear Equations and Inequalities in One Variable

a. Thing
b. Element0
c. Undefined
d. Undefined

97. In mathematics, the _____ , or members of a set or more generally a class are all those objects which when collected together make up the set or class.
   a. Elements0
   b. Thing
   c. Undefined
   d. Undefined

98. In mathematics and more specifically set theory, the _____ set is the unique set which contains no elements.
   a. Thing
   b. Empty0
   c. Undefined
   d. Undefined

99. _____ are objects, characters, or other concrete representations of ideas, concepts, or other abstractions.
   a. Symbols0
   b. Thing
   c. Undefined
   d. Undefined

100. A _____ is a numeral used to indicate a count. The most common use of the word today is to name the part of a fraction that tells the number or count of equal parts.
   a. Numerator0
   b. Thing
   c. Undefined
   d. Undefined

101. _____ is the ability to hold, receive or absorb, or a measure thereof, similar to the concept of volume.
   a. Concept
   b. Capacity0
   c. Undefined
   d. Undefined

102. Compass and straightedge or ruler-and-compass _____ is the _____ of lengths or angles using only an idealized ruler and compass.
   a. Thing
   b. Construction0
   c. Undefined
   d. Undefined

103. In classical geometry, a _____ of a circle or sphere is any line segment from its center to its boundary. By extension, the _____ of a circle or sphere is the length of any such segment. The _____ is half the diameter. In science and engineering the term _____ of curvature is commonly used as a synonym for _____.
   a. Radius0
   b. Thing
   c. Undefined
   d. Undefined

104. A _____ is a fee added to a customer's bill.
   a. Service charge0
   b. Thing
   c. Undefined
   d. Undefined

105. In mathematics, a _____ number is a number which can be expressed as a ratio of two integers. Non-integer _____ numbers (commonly called fractions) are usually written as the vulgar fraction a / b, where b is not zero.
   a. Thing
   b. Rational0
   c. Undefined
   d. Undefined

106. In physics, _____ is an influence that may cause an object to accelerate. It may be experienced as a lift, a push, or a pull. The actual acceleration of the body is determined by the vector sum of all forces acting on it, known as net _____ or resultant _____.
   a. Force0
   b. Thing
   c. Undefined
   d. Undefined

107. _____, from Latin meaning "to make progress", is defined in two different ways. Pure economic _____ is the increase in wealth that an investor has from making an investment, taking into consideration all costs associated with that investment including the opportunity cost of capital.
   a. Profit0
   b. Thing
   c. Undefined
   d. Undefined

Chapter 3. Problem Solving

1. _____ is the fee paid on borrowed money.
   a. Interest0
   b. Thing
   c. Undefined
   d. Undefined

2. _____ is a kind of property which exists as magnitude or multitude. It is among the basic classes of things along with quality, substance, change, and relation.
   a. Thing
   b. Amount0
   c. Undefined
   d. Undefined

3. A _____ is a special kind of ratio, indicating a relationship between two measurements with different units, such as miles to gallons or cents to pounds.
   a. Rate0
   b. Thing
   c. Undefined
   d. Undefined

4. _____ is a way of expressing a number as a fraction of 100 per cent meaning "per hundred".
   a. Thing
   b. Percent0
   c. Undefined
   d. Undefined

5. An _____ is the fee paid on borrow money.
   a. Concept
   b. Interest rate0
   c. Undefined
   d. Undefined

6. A _____ are accounts maintained by commercial banks, savings and loan associations, credit unions, and mutual savings banks that pay interest but can not be used directly as money by, for example, writing a cheque.
   a. Thing
   b. Savings account0
   c. Undefined
   d. Undefined

7. _____ forms part of thinking. Considered the most complex of all intellectual functions, _____ has been defined as higher-order cognitive process that requires the modulation and control of more routine or fundamental skills.
   a. Problem solving0
   b. Thing
   c. Undefined
   d. Undefined

8. A _____ is a negotiable instrument instructing a financial institution to pay a specific amount of a specific currency from a specific demand account held in the maker/depositor's name with that institution. Both the maker and payee may be natural persons or legal entities.
   a. Thing
   b. Check0
   c. Undefined
   d. Undefined

9. In mathematics, a _____ is the result of multiplying, or an expression that identifies factors to be multiplied.
   a. Thing
   b. Product0
   c. Undefined
   d. Undefined

10. In mathematics, and in particular in abstract algebra, the _____ is a property of binary operations that generalises the distributive law from elementary algebra.
    a. Thing
    b. Distributive property0
    c. Undefined
    d. Undefined

11. In chemistry, a _____ is substance made by combining two or more different materials in such a way that no chemical reaction occurs.
   a. Mixture0
   b. Thing
   c. Undefined
   d. Undefined

12. A _____ is the result of the addition of a set of numbers. The numbers may be natural numbers, complex numbers, matrices, or still more complicated objects. An infinite _____ is a subtle procedure known as a series.
   a. Thing
   b. Sum0
   c. Undefined
   d. Undefined

13. In mathematics, an _____, mean, or central tendency of a data set refers to a measure of the "middle" or "expected" value of the data set.
   a. Concept
   b. Average0
   c. Undefined
   d. Undefined

14. A _____ is a unit of length, usually used to measure distance, in a number of different systems, including Imperial units, United States customary units and Norwegian/Swedish mil. Its size can vary from system to system, but in each is between 1 and 10 kilometers. In contemporary English contexts _____ refers to either:
   a. Thing
   b. Mile0
   c. Undefined
   d. Undefined

15. In mathematics, a _____ is a two-dimensional manifold or surface that is perfectly flat.
   a. Plane0
   b. Thing
   c. Undefined
   d. Undefined

16. _____ is a unit of speed, expressing the number of international miles covered per hour.
   a. Miles per hour0
   b. Thing
   c. Undefined
   d. Undefined

17. In mathematics, the additive inverse, or _____ of a number n is the number that, when added to n, yields zero. The additive inverse of n is denoted −n. For example, 7 is −7, because 7 + (−7) = 0, and the additive inverse of −0.3 is 0.3, because −0.3 + 0.3 = 0.
   a. Opposite0
   b. Thing
   c. Undefined
   d. Undefined

18. In mathematics, _____ are two-dimensional manifolds or surfaces that are perfectly flat.
   a. Thing
   b. Planes0
   c. Undefined
   d. Undefined

19. In mathematics, the _____ of a number n is the number that, when added to n, yields zero. The _____ of n is denoted −n. For example, 7 is −7, because 7 + (−7) = 0, and the _____ of −0.3 is 0.3, because −0.3 + 0.3 = 0.
   a. Thing
   b. Additive inverse0
   c. Undefined
   d. Undefined

20. A _____ is a deliberate process for transforming one or more inputs into one or more results.

a. Thing
b. Calculation0
c. Undefined
d. Undefined

21. A _____ is a method of using property as security for the payment of a debt.
   a. Mortgage0
   b. Thing
   c. Undefined
   d. Undefined

22. A _____ is a system of payment named after the small plastic card issued to users of the system.
   a. Credit card0
   b. Thing
   c. Undefined
   d. Undefined

23. A _____ is a type of debt. All material things can be lent but this article focuses exclusively on monetary loans. Like all debt instruments, a _____ entails the redistribution of financial assets over time, between the lender and the borrower.
   a. Loan0
   b. Thing
   c. Undefined
   d. Undefined

24. _____ finance, in finance, a debt security, issued by Issuer
   a. Thing
   b. Bond0
   c. Undefined
   d. Undefined

25. A _____ or CD is a time deposit, a financial product commonly offered to consumers by banks, thrift institutions, and credit unions.
   a. Certificate of deposit0
   b. Thing
   c. Undefined
   d. Undefined

26. Multiple Signal Classification, also known as _____, is an algorithm used for frequency estimation and emitter location.
   a. Music0
   b. Thing
   c. Undefined
   d. Undefined

27. In botany, _____ are above-ground plant organs specialized for photosynthesis. Their characteristics are typically analyzed by using Fiobonacci's sequences.
   a. Thing
   b. Leaves0
   c. Undefined
   d. Undefined

28. A _____ is the part of the dividend that is left over when the dividend is not evenly divisible by the divisor.
   a. Remainder0
   b. Thing
   c. Undefined
   d. Undefined

29. In plane geometry, a _____ is a polygon with four equal sides, four right angles, and parallel opposite sides. In algebra, the _____ of a number is that number multiplied by itself.
   a. Square0
   b. Thing
   c. Undefined
   d. Undefined

30. _____ is a special mathematical relationship between two quantities. Two quantities are called proportional if they vary in such a way that one of the quantities is a constant multiple of the other, or equivalently if they have a constant ratio.
   a. Thing
   b. Proportionality0
   c. Undefined
   d. Undefined

31. A _____ is a quantity that denotes the proportional amount or magnitude of one quantity relative to another.
   a. Thing
   b. Ratio0
   c. Undefined
   d. Undefined

32. In mathematical logic, a Gödel numbering (or Gödel _____) is a function that assigns to each symbol and well-formed formula of some formal language a unique natural number called its Gödel number.
   a. Code0
   b. Thing
   c. Undefined
   d. Undefined

33. The _____, the average in everyday English, which is also called the arithmetic _____ (and is distinguished from the geometric _____ or harmonic _____). The average is also called the sample _____. The expected value of a random variable, which is also called the population _____.
   a. Thing
   b. Mean0
   c. Undefined
   d. Undefined

34. The _____ are the only integral domain whose positive elements are well-ordered, and in which order is preserved by addition. Like the natural numbers, the _____ form a countably infinite set. The set of all _____ is usually denoted in mathematics by a boldface Z .
   a. Integers0
   b. Thing
   c. Undefined
   d. Undefined

35. In sociology and biology a _____ is the collection of people or organisms of a particular species living in a given geographic area or space, usually measured by a census.
   a. Thing
   b. Population0
   c. Undefined
   d. Undefined

36. The _____ (symbol _____) and the millibar (symbol mbar, also mb) are units of pressure.
   a. Thing
   b. Bar0
   c. Undefined
   d. Undefined

37. A bar chart, also known as a _____, is a chart with rectangular bars of lengths usually proportional to the magnitudes or frequencies of what they represent.
   a. Bar graph0
   b. Thing
   c. Undefined
   d. Undefined

38. _____ (or proportionality) are two quantities that vary in such a way that one of the quatities is a constant multiple of the other, or equivalently if they have a constant ratio.
   a. Thing
   b. Proportions0
   c. Undefined
   d. Undefined

39. In common philosophical language, a proposition or _____, is the content of an assertion, that is, it is true-or-false and defined by the meaning of a particular piece of language.
   a. Statement0
   b. Concept
   c. Undefined
   d. Undefined

40. A _____ is the part of a fraction that tells how many equal parts make up a whole, and which is used in the name of the fraction: "halves", "thirds", "fourths" or "quarters", "fifths" and so on.
   a. Denominator0
   b. Concept
   c. Undefined
   d. Undefined

41. _____ is a binary operation on two vectors in a three-dimensional Euclidean space that results in another vector which is perpedicular to the two input vectors.
   a. Cross product0
   b. Thing
   c. Undefined
   d. Undefined

42. A _____ signifies a point or points of probability on a subject e.g., the _____ of creativity, which allows for the formation of rule or norm or law by interpretation of the phenomena events that can be created.
   a. Thing
   b. Principle0
   c. Undefined
   d. Undefined

43. The _____ of measurement are a globally standardized and modernized form of the metric system.
   a. Units0
   b. Thing
   c. Undefined
   d. Undefined

44. _____ is the part of statistical practice concerned with the selection of individual observations intended to yield some knowledge about a population of concern, especially for the purposes of statistical inference.
   a. Thing
   b. Sampling0
   c. Undefined
   d. Undefined

45. _____ refers to all non-domesticated plants, animals, and other organisms.
   a. Thing
   b. Wildlife0
   c. Undefined
   d. Undefined

46. _____ is a subset of a population.
   a. Thing
   b. Sample0
   c. Undefined
   d. Undefined

47. The act of _____ is the calculated approximation of a result which is usable even if input data may be incomplete, uncertain, or noisy.
   a. Estimating0
   b. Thing
   c. Undefined
   d. Undefined

48. In mathematics, two quantities are called _____ if they vary in such a way that one of the quantities is a constant multiple of the other, or equivalently if they have a constant ratio.

a. Proportional0
b. Thing
c. Undefined
d. Undefined

49. _____ is the distance around a given two-dimensional object. As a general rule, the _____ of a polygon can always be calculated by adding all the length of the sides together. So, the formula for triangles is P = a + b + c, where a, b and c stand for each side of it. For quadrilaterals the equation is P = a + b + c + d. For equilateral polygons, P = na, where n is the number of sides and a is the side length.
   a. Perimeter0
   b. Thing
   c. Undefined
   d. Undefined

50. In Euclidean geometry, a _____ is the set of all points in a plane at a fixed distance, called the radius, from a given point, the center.
   a. Circle0
   b. Thing
   c. Undefined
   d. Undefined

51. The _____ is the distance around a closed curve. _____ is a kind of perimeter.
   a. Circumference0
   b. Thing
   c. Undefined
   d. Undefined

52. A pair of angles is _____ if their respective measures sum to 180 degrees.
   a. Concept
   b. Supplementary0
   c. Undefined
   d. Undefined

53. A pair of angles are _____ if the sum of their angles is 90°.
   a. Concept
   b. Complementary0
   c. Undefined
   d. Undefined

54. _____ are external two-dimensional outlines, with the appearance or configuration of some thing - in contrast to the matter or content or substance of which it is composed.
   a. Shapes0
   b. Thing
   c. Undefined
   d. Undefined

55. _____ is a set, with some particular properties and usually some additional structure, such as the operations of addition or multiplication, for instance.
   a. Space0
   b. Thing
   c. Undefined
   d. Undefined

56. The _____ of a solid object is the three-dimensional concept of how much space it occupies, often quantified numerically.
   a. Volume0
   b. Thing
   c. Undefined
   d. Undefined

57. A _____, is a symbolized depiction of space which highlights relations between components of that space. Most usually a _____ is a two-dimensional, geometrically accurate representation of a three-dimensional space.

Chapter 3. Problem Solving

    a. Thing   b. Map0
    c. Undefined   d. Undefined

58. In geometry, a _____ is the intersection of a body in 2-dimensional space with a line, or of a body in 3-dimensional space with a plane
    a. Cross section0   b. Thing
    c. Undefined   d. Undefined

59. In physics, _____ are surface waves on a liquid with wavelengths so short that the liquid's motion is governed almost entirely by surface tension forces.
    a. Ripples0   b. Thing
    c. Undefined   d. Undefined

60. In geometry, the _____ of an object is a point in some sense in the middle of the object.
    a. Thing   b. Center0
    c. Undefined   d. Undefined

61. In geometry, a line _____ is a part of a line that is bounded by two end points, and contains every point on the line between its end points.
    a. Concept   b. Segment0
    c. Undefined   d. Undefined

62. In classical geometry, a _____ of a circle or sphere is any line segment from its center to its boundary. By extension, the _____ of a circle or sphere is the length of any such segment. The _____ is half the diameter. In science and engineering the term _____ of curvature is commonly used as a synonym for _____.
    a. Thing   b. Radius0
    c. Undefined   d. Undefined

63. A _____ is a part of a line that is bounded by two end points, and contains every point on the line between its end points.
    a. Thing   b. Line segment0
    c. Undefined   d. Undefined

64. In geometry, an _____ is a point at which a line segment or ray terminates.
    a. Thing   b. Endpoint0
    c. Undefined   d. Undefined

65. In geometry, a _____ (Greek words diairo = divide and metro = measure) of a circle is any straight line segment that passes through the centre and whose endpoints are on the circular boundary, or, in more modern usage, the length of such a line segment. When using the word in the more modern sense, one speaks of the _____ rather than a _____, because all diameters of a circle have the same length. This length is twice the radius. The _____ of a circle is also the longest chord that the circle has.
    a. Diameter0   b. Thing
    c. Undefined   d. Undefined

66. The word _____ comes from the Latin word linearis, which means created by lines.

a. Thing
b. Linear0
c. Undefined
d. Undefined

67. A _____ is a function that assigns a number to subsets of a given set.
a. Thing
b. Measure0
c. Undefined
d. Undefined

68. A _____ is a three-dimensional solid object bounded by six square faces, facets, or sides, with three meeting at each vertex.
a. Cube0
b. Thing
c. Undefined
d. Undefined

69. In mathematics, a _____ is a quadric surface, with the following equation in Cartesian coordinates: $(x/_a)^2 + (y/_b)^2 = 1$.
a. Cylinder0
b. Thing
c. Undefined
d. Undefined

70. A _____ is a three-dimensional geometric shape formed by straight lines through a fixed point (vertex) to the points of a fixed curve (directrix)
a. Cone0
b. Concept
c. Undefined
d. Undefined

71. In mathematics, an inequality is a statement about the relative size or order of two objects. For example 14 > 10, or 14 is _____ 10.
a. Thing
b. Greater than0
c. Undefined
d. Undefined

72. In mathematics, a _____ is the set of all points in three-dimensional space (R^3) which are at distance r from a fixed point of that space, where r is a positive real number called the radius of the _____. The fixed point is called the center or centre, and is not part of the _____ itself.
a. Sphere0
b. Thing
c. Undefined
d. Undefined

73. A _____ is one of the basic shapes of geometry: a polygon with three vertices and three sides which are straight line segments.
a. Thing
b. Triangle0
c. Undefined
d. Undefined

74. Compass and straightedge or ruler-and-compass _____ is the _____ of lengths or angles using only an idealized ruler and compass.
a. Thing
b. Construction0
c. Undefined
d. Undefined

75. In mathematics, suppose C is a collection of mathematical objects . Then we say that C is _____ if every c ∊ C is uniquely determined by less information about c than one would expect.

Chapter 3. Problem Solving

    a. Thing
    c. Undefined
    b. Rigid0
    d. Undefined

76. A _____ given two distinct points A and B on the _____, is the set of points C on the line containing points A and B such that A is not strictly between C and B.
    a. Thing
    c. Undefined
    b. Ray0
    d. Undefined

77. In geometry and physics, _____ are half-lines that continue forever in one direction.
    a. Thing
    c. Undefined
    b. Rays0
    d. Undefined

78. In geometry, a _____ is a special kind of point, usually a corner of a polygon, polyhedron, or higher dimensional polytope. In the geometry of curves a _____ is a point of where the first derivative of curvature is zero. In graph theory, a _____ is the fundamental unit out of which graphs are formed
    a. Thing
    c. Undefined
    b. Vertex0
    d. Undefined

79. In mathematics, there are several meanings of _____ depending on the subject.
    a. Thing
    c. Undefined
    b. Degree0
    d. Undefined

80. A _____ is a movement of an object in a circular motion. A two-dimensional object rotates around a center (or point) of _____. A three-dimensional object rotates around a line called an axis. If the axis of _____ is within the body, the body is said to rotate upon itself, or spin—which implies relative speed and perhaps free-movement with angular momentum. A circular motion about an external point, e.g. the Earth about the Sun, is called an orbit or more properly an orbital revolution.
    a. Thing
    c. Undefined
    b. Rotation0
    d. Undefined

81. In set theory and other branches of mathematics, two kinds of complements are defined, the relative _____ and the absolute _____.
    a. Thing
    c. Undefined
    b. Complement0
    d. Undefined

82. A _____ is a quadrilateral, which is defined as a shape with four sides, which has a pair of parallel sides.
    a. Thing
    c. Undefined
    b. Trapezoid0
    d. Undefined

83. In geometry, a _____ is defined as a quadrilateral where all four of its angles are right angles.
    a. Rectangle0
    c. Undefined
    b. Thing
    d. Undefined

84. In mathematics, a _____ is an n-tuple with n being 3.

a. Thing
b. Triple0
c. Undefined
d. Undefined

85. In mathematics, _____ geometry was the traditional name for the geometry of three-dimensional Euclidean space — for practical purposes the kind of space we live in.
   a. Solid0
   b. Thing
   c. Undefined
   d. Undefined

86. In business, particularly accounting, a _____ is the time intervals that the accounts, statement, payments, or other calculations cover.
   a. Thing
   b. Period0
   c. Undefined
   d. Undefined

87. The metre (or _____, see spelling differences) is a measure of length. It is the basic unit of length in the metric system and in the International System of Units (SI), used around the world for general and scientific purposes.
   a. Concept
   b. Meter0
   c. Undefined
   d. Undefined

88. U.S. liquid _____ is legally defined as 231 cubic inches, and is equal to 3.785411784 litres or abotu 0.13368 cubic feet. This is the most common definition of a _____. The U.S. fluid ounce is defined as 1/128 of a U.S. _____.
   a. Gallon0
   b. Thing
   c. Undefined
   d. Undefined

89. In Euclidean geometry, a uniform _____ is a linear transformation that enlargers or diminishes objects, and whose _____ factor is the same in all directions. This is also called homothethy.
   a. Thing
   b. Scale0
   c. Undefined
   d. Undefined

90. A _____ is 360° or 2δ radians.
   a. Turn0
   b. Thing
   c. Undefined
   d. Undefined

91. In mathematics, a matrix can be thought of as each row or _____ being a vector. Hence, a space formed by row vectors or _____ vectors are said to be a row space or a _____ space.
   a. Concept
   b. Column0
   c. Undefined
   d. Undefined

92. _____ or investing is a term with several closely-related meanings in business management, finance and economics, related to saving or deferring consumption.
   a. Investment0
   b. Thing
   c. Undefined
   d. Undefined

93. An _____ is a combination of numbers, operators, grouping symbols and/or free variables and bound variables arranged in a meaningful way which can be evaluated..

Chapter 3. Problem Solving

a. Expression0
b. Thing
c. Undefined
d. Undefined

94. Regrouping is the act of putting ones into groups of 10. For example, the 1 on the far right of 131 would be denoted _____ if the digit of the number being subtracted is larger than 1, such as 131-99.
    a. Thing
    b. By 100
    c. Undefined
    d. Undefined

95. _____ is the largest city in the state of Texas and the fourth-largest in the United States. As of the 2005 U.S. Census estimate, it had a population of more than 2 million.
    a. Thing
    b. Houston0
    c. Undefined
    d. Undefined

96. _____ is a state located in the southern and southwestern regions of the United States of America.
    a. Texas0
    b. Thing
    c. Undefined
    d. Undefined

97. _____ are a measure of time.
    a. Minutes0
    b. Thing
    c. Undefined
    d. Undefined

98. _____, in economics and political economy, are the distributions or payments awarded to the various suppliers of the factors of production.
    a. Returns0
    b. Thing
    c. Undefined
    d. Undefined

99. In mathematics, a _____ can mean either an element of the set {1, 2, 3, ...} (i.e the positive integers or the counting numbers) or an element of the set {0, 1, 2, 3, ...} (i.e. the non-negative integers).
    a. Thing
    b. Natural number0
    c. Undefined
    d. Undefined

100. _____ is a physical property of a system that underlies the common notions of hot and cold; something that is hotter has the greater _____.
    a. Temperature0
    b. Thing
    c. Undefined
    d. Undefined

101. Mathematical _____ is used to represent ideas.
    a. Notation0
    b. Thing
    c. Undefined
    d. Undefined

102. A _____ is a one-dimensional picture in which the integers are shown as specially-marked points evenly spaced on a line.
    a. Thing
    b. Number line0
    c. Undefined
    d. Undefined

103. A _____ is a set of possible values that a variable can take on in order to satisfy a given set of conditions, which may include equations and inequalities.
- a. Solution set0
- b. Thing
- c. Undefined
- d. Undefined

104. A _____ is a landform that extends above the surrounding terrain in a limited area. A _____ is generally steeper than a hill, but there is no universally accepted standard definition for the height of a _____ or a hill although a _____ usually has an identifiable summit.
- a. Mountain0
- b. Thing
- c. Undefined
- d. Undefined

105. A _____ is a symbolic representation denoting a quantity or expression. It often represents an "unknown" quantity that has the potential to change.
- a. Thing
- b. Variable0
- c. Undefined
- d. Undefined

Chapter 4. Linear Equations and inequalities in Two Variables

1. A _____ is a unit of length, usually used to measure distance, in a number of different systems, including Imperial units, United States customary units and Norwegian/Swedish mil. Its size can vary from system to system, but in each is between 1 and 10 kilometers. In contemporary English contexts _____ refers to either:
   a. Thing
   b. Mile0
   c. Undefined
   d. Undefined

2. U.S. liquid _____ is legally defined as 231 cubic inches, and is equal to 3.785411784 litres or abotu 0.13368 cubic feet. This is the most common definition of a _____. The U.S. fluid ounce is defined as 1/128 of a U.S. _____.
   a. Thing
   b. Gallon0
   c. Undefined
   d. Undefined

3. A _____ is a symbolic representation denoting a quantity or expression. It often represents an "unknown" quantity that has the potential to change.
   a. Variable0
   b. Thing
   c. Undefined
   d. Undefined

4. In mathematics, an _____, mean, or central tendency of a data set refers to a measure of the "middle" or "expected" value of the data set.
   a. Concept
   b. Average0
   c. Undefined
   d. Undefined

5. A _____ is a set of numbers that designate location in a given reference system, such as x,y in a planar _____ system or an x,y,z in a three-dimensional _____ system.
   a. Coordinate0
   b. Thing
   c. Undefined
   d. Undefined

6. In mathematics and its applications, a _____ is a system for assigning an n-tuple of numbers or scalars to each point in an n-dimensional space.
   a. Coordinate system0
   b. Concept
   c. Undefined
   d. Undefined

7. _____ are the basic objects of study in graph theory. Informally speaking, a graph is a set of objects called points, nodes, or vertices connected by links called lines or edges.
   a. Thing
   b. Graphs0
   c. Undefined
   d. Undefined

8. The word _____ comes from the Latin word linearis, which means created by lines.
   a. Thing
   b. Linear0
   c. Undefined
   d. Undefined

9. A _____ is an equation in which each term is either a constant or the product of a constant times the first power of a variable.
   a. Linear equation0
   b. Thing
   c. Undefined
   d. Undefined

10. An _____ is a collection of two not necessarily distinct objects, one of which is distinguished as the first coordinate and the other as the second coordinate.

Chapter 4. Linear Equations and inequalities in Two Variables

    a. Thing
    c. Undefined
    b. Ordered pair0
    d. Undefined

11. A _____ is the result of the addition of a set of numbers. The numbers may be natural numbers, complex numbers, matrices, or still more complicated objects. An infinite _____ is a subtle procedure known as a series.
    a. Sum0
    c. Undefined
    b. Thing
    d. Undefined

12. In mathematics, the conjugate _____ or adjoint matrix of an m-by-n matrix A with complex entries is the n-by-m matrix A* obtained from A by taking the transpose and then taking the complex conjugate of each entry.
    a. Pairs0
    c. Undefined
    b. Thing
    d. Undefined

13. In common philosophical language, a proposition or _____, is the content of an assertion, that is, it is true-or-false and defined by the meaning of a particular piece of language.
    a. Statement0
    c. Undefined
    b. Concept
    d. Undefined

14. A _____ is a negotiable instrument instructing a financial institution to pay a specific amount of a specific currency from a specific demand account held in the maker/depositor's name with that institution. Both the maker and payee may be natural persons or legal entities.
    a. Thing
    c. Undefined
    b. Check0
    d. Undefined

15. In mathematics, the concept of a _____ tries to capture the intuitive idea of a geometrical one-dimensional and continuous object. A simple example is the circle.
    a. Curve0
    c. Undefined
    b. Thing
    d. Undefined

16. The _____ are the only integral domain whose positive elements are well-ordered, and in which order is preserved by addition. Like the natural numbers, the _____ form a countably infinite set. The set of all _____ is usually denoted in mathematics by a boldface Z .
    a. Thing
    c. Undefined
    b. Integers0
    d. Undefined

17. In mathematics and the mathematical sciences, a _____ is a fixed, but possibly unspecified, value. This is in contrast to a variable, which is not fixed.
    a. Constant0
    c. Undefined
    b. Thing
    d. Undefined

18. A _____ is a number that is less than zero.
    a. Thing
    c. Undefined
    b. Negative number0
    d. Undefined

19. The _____ of measurement are a globally standardized and modernized form of the metric system.

Chapter 4. Linear Equations and inequalities in Two Variables

a. Units0
b. Thing
c. Undefined
d. Undefined

20. A _____ of a number is the product of that number with any integer.
    a. Thing
    b. Multiple0
    c. Undefined
    d. Undefined

21. In mathematics, a _____ is a constant multiplicative factor of a certain object. The object can be such things as a variable, a vector, a function, etc. For example, the _____ of $9x^2$ is 9.
    a. Thing
    b. Coefficient0
    c. Undefined
    d. Undefined

22. A _____ is the part of a fraction that tells how many equal parts make up a whole, and which is used in the name of the fraction: "halves", "thirds", "fourths" or "quarters", "fifths" and so on.
    a. Denominator0
    b. Concept
    c. Undefined
    d. Undefined

23. In mathematics, a _____ (also spelled reflexion) is a map that transforms an object into its mirror image.
    a. Reflection0
    b. Concept
    c. Undefined
    d. Undefined

24. A _____ consists of one quarter of the coordinate plane.
    a. Quadrant0
    b. Thing
    c. Undefined
    d. Undefined

25. The _____ integers are all the integers from zero on upwards.
    a. Thing
    b. Nonnegative0
    c. Undefined
    d. Undefined

26. In mathematics, the _____ of a coordinate system is the point where the axes of the system intersect.
    a. Origin0
    b. Thing
    c. Undefined
    d. Undefined

27. The _____, the average in everyday English, which is also called the arithmetic _____ (and is distinguished from the geometric _____ or harmonic _____). The average is also called the sample _____. The expected value of a random variable, which is also called the population _____.
    a. Mean0
    b. Thing
    c. Undefined
    d. Undefined

28. In mathematics, the _____ of two sets A and B is the set that contains all elements of A that also belong to B (or equivalently, all elements of B that also belong to A), but no other elements.
    a. Intersection0
    b. Thing
    c. Undefined
    d. Undefined

29. In Euclidean geometry, a uniform _____ is a linear transformation that enlargers or diminishes objects, and whose _____ factor is the same in all directions. This is also called homothethy.

a. Scale0 b. Thing
c. Undefined d. Undefined

30. In geometry, a _____ is defined as a quadrilateral where all four of its angles are right angles.
a. Rectangle0 b. Thing
c. Undefined d. Undefined

31. An _____ is when two lines intersect somewhere on a plane creating a right angle at intersection
a. Axes0 b. Thing
c. Undefined d. Undefined

32. _____ means in succession or back-to-back
a. Thing b. Consecutive0
c. Undefined d. Undefined

33. In plane geometry, a _____ is a polygon with four equal sides, four right angles, and parallel opposite sides. In algebra, the _____ of a number is that number multiplied by itself.
a. Thing b. Square0
c. Undefined d. Undefined

34. In mathematics, a _____ is a two-dimensional manifold or surface that is perfectly flat.
a. Thing b. Plane0
c. Undefined d. Undefined

35. In mathematics, _____ is a part of the set theoretic notion of function.
a. Image0 b. Thing
c. Undefined d. Undefined

36. In mathematics, a _____ is any one of several different types of functions, mappings, operations, or transformations.
a. Thing b. Projection0
c. Undefined d. Undefined

37. In sociology and biology a _____ is the collection of people or organisms of a particular species living in a given geographic area or space, usually measured by a census.
a. Thing b. Population0
c. Undefined d. Undefined

38. A _____ is a special kind of ratio, indicating a relationship between two measurements with different units, such as miles to gallons or cents to pounds.
a. Thing b. Rate0
c. Undefined d. Undefined

39. _____ is a synonym for information.

Chapter 4. Linear Equations and inequalities in Two Variables

a. Thing
b. Data0
c. Undefined
d. Undefined

40. Fixed costs are expenses whose total does not change in proportion to the activity of a business.Unit fixed costs decline with volume following a retangular hyperbola as the volume of production.Variable costs by contrast change in relation to the activity of a business such as sales or production volume.Along with variable costs,fixed costs make up one of the two components of total cost. In the most simple production function total cost is equal to fixed costs plus variable costs.In accounting terminology, fixed costs will broadly include all costs which are not included in cost of goods sold, and variable costs are those captured in costs of goods sold. The implicit assumption required to make the equivalence between the accounting and economics terminology is that the accounting period is equal to the period in which fixed costs do not vary in relation to production. In practice, this equivalence does not always hold and depending on the period under consideration by management, some overhead expenses can be adjusted by management, and the specific allocation of each expense to each category will be decided under cost accounting.In business planning and management accounting, usage of the terms fixed costs, variable costs and others will often differ from usage in economics, and may depend on the intended use. For example, costs may be segregated into per unit costs fixed costs per period, and variable costs as a proportion of revenue. Capital expenditures will usually be allocated separately, and depending on the purpose, a portion may be regularly allocated to expenses as depreciation and amortization and seen as a _____ per period, or the entire amount may be considered upfront fixed costs.

a. Fixed cost0
b. Thing
c. Undefined
d. Undefined

41. _____ are expenses whose total does not change in proportion to the activity of a business, within the relevant time period or scale of production

a. Fixed costs0
b. Thing
c. Undefined
d. Undefined

42. _____ is the level of functional and/or metabolic efficiency of an organism at both the micro level.

a. Thing
b. Health0
c. Undefined
d. Undefined

43. In mathematics, the _____ of a function is the set of all "output" values produced by that function. Given a function $f: A \to B$, the _____ of f, is defined to be the set $\{x \in B : x = f(a) \text{ for some } a \in A\}$.

a. Thing
b. Range0
c. Undefined
d. Undefined

44. In geographic information systems, a _____ comprises an entity with a geographic location, typically determined by points, arcs, or polygons. Carriageways and cadastres exemplify _____ data.

a. Thing
b. Feature0
c. Undefined
d. Undefined

45. Any point where a graph makes contact with an coordinate axis is called an _____ of the graph

a. Thing
b. Intercept0
c. Undefined
d. Undefined

46. In astronomy, geography, geometry and related sciences and contexts, a plane is said to be _____ at a given point if it is locally perpendicular to the gradient of the gravity field, i.e., with the direction of the gravitational force at that point.

Chapter 4. Linear Equations and inequalities in Two Variables

  a. Thing   b. Horizontal0
  c. Undefined   d. Undefined

47. In business, particularly accounting, a _____ is the time intervals that the accounts, statement, payments, or other calculations cover.
  a. Period0   b. Thing
  c. Undefined   d. Undefined

48. The metre (or _____, see spelling differences) is a measure of length. It is the basic unit of length in the metric system and in the International System of Units (SI), used around the world for general and scientific purposes.
  a. Meter0   b. Concept
  c. Undefined   d. Undefined

49. _____ is a branch of mathematics concerning the study of structure, relation and quantity.
  a. Concept   b. Algebra0
  c. Undefined   d. Undefined

50. _____ is a physical property of a system that underlies the common notions of hot and cold; something that is hotter has the greater _____.
  a. Thing   b. Temperature0
  c. Undefined   d. Undefined

51. In geometry, a line _____ is a part of a line that is bounded by two end points, and contains every point on the line between its end points.
  a. Segment0   b. Concept
  c. Undefined   d. Undefined

52. _____ is often used to describe the measurement of the steepness, incline, gradient, or grade of a straight line. The _____ is defined as the ratio of the "rise" divided by the "run" between two points on a line, or in other words, the ratio of the altitude change to the horizontal distance between any two points on the line.
  a. Slope0   b. Thing
  c. Undefined   d. Undefined

53. A _____ is a function that assigns a number to subsets of a given set.
  a. Thing   b. Measure0
  c. Undefined   d. Undefined

54. Mathematical _____ is used to represent ideas.
  a. Notation0   b. Thing
  c. Undefined   d. Undefined

55. A _____ is a quantity that denotes the proportional amount or magnitude of one quantity relative to another.
  a. Ratio0   b. Thing
  c. Undefined   d. Undefined

Chapter 4. Linear Equations and inequalities in Two Variables

56. A _____ is a numeral used to indicate a count. The most common use of the word today is to name the part of a fraction that tells the number or count of equal parts.
   a. Thing
   b. Numerator0
   c. Undefined
   d. Undefined

57. In mathematics, defined and _____ are used to explain whether or not expressions have meaningful, sensible, and unambiguous values.
   a. Undefined0
   b. Thing
   c. Undefined
   d. Undefined

58. The existence and properties of _____ are the basis of Euclid's parallel postulate. _____ are two lines on the same plane that do not intersect even assuming that lines extend to infinity in either direction.
   a. Parallel lines0
   b. Thing
   c. Undefined
   d. Undefined

59. A _____ is a part of a line that is bounded by two end points, and contains every point on the line between its end points.
   a. Line segment0
   b. Thing
   c. Undefined
   d. Undefined

60. _____ is a trigonemtric function that is important when studying triangles and modeling periodic phenomena, among other applications.
   a. Thing
   b. Sine0
   c. Undefined
   d. Undefined

61. In mathematics, a subset of Euclidean space R^n is called _____ if it is closed and bounded.
   a. Thing
   b. Compact0
   c. Undefined
   d. Undefined

62. In mathematics, the _____ (or modulus) of a real number is its numerical value without regard to its sign.
   a. Absolute value0
   b. Thing
   c. Undefined
   d. Undefined

63. Compass and straightedge or ruler-and-compass _____ is the _____ of lengths or angles using only an idealized ruler and compass.
   a. Construction0
   b. Thing
   c. Undefined
   d. Undefined

64. In linear algebra, the _____ of an n-by-n square matrix A is defined to be the sum of the elements on the main diagonal of A,
   a. Thing
   b. Trace0
   c. Undefined
   d. Undefined

65. A _____ is a one-dimensional picture in which the integers are shown as specially-marked points evenly spaced on a line.

Chapter 4. Linear Equations and inequalities in Two Variables

a. Number line0
b. Thing
c. Undefined
d. Undefined

66. A _____ is a set of possible values that a variable can take on in order to satisfy a given set of conditions, which may include equations and inequalities.
a. Thing
b. Solution set0
c. Undefined
d. Undefined

67. A _____ is an abstract model that uses mathematical language to describe the behavior of a system. Eykhoff defined a _____ as 'a representation of the essential aspects of an existing system which presents knowledge of that system in usable form'.
a. Mathematical model0
b. Thing
c. Undefined
d. Undefined

68. In geometry, the _____ of an object is a point in some sense in the middle of the object.
a. Thing
b. Center0
c. Undefined
d. Undefined

69. _____ is a fixed, but possibly unspecified, value. This is in contrast to a variable, which is not fixed.
a. Thing
b. Constant term0
c. Undefined
d. Undefined

70. A _____ is a tool similar to a ruler, but without markings.
a. Thing
b. Straightedge0
c. Undefined
d. Undefined

71. _____ is a form of periodic payment from an employer to an employee, which is specified in an employment contract.
a. Thing
b. Gross pay0
c. Undefined
d. Undefined

72. A _____ is a form of periodic payment from an employer to an employee, which is specified in an employment contract.
a. Thing
b. Salary0
c. Undefined
d. Undefined

73. Equivalence is the condition of being _____ or essentially equal.
a. Thing
b. Equivalent0
c. Undefined
d. Undefined

74. A _____, scatter diagram or scatter graph is a chart that uses Cartesian coordinates to display values for two variables.
a. Scatter plot0
b. Thing
c. Undefined
d. Undefined

Chapter 4. Linear Equations and inequalities in Two Variables

75. A _____ is a statement or claimt that a particular event will occur in the future in more certain terms than a forecast.
    a. Thing
    b. Prediction0
    c. Undefined
    d. Undefined

76. In mathematics, and in particular in abstract algebra, the _____ is a property of binary operations that generalises the distributive law from elementary algebra.
    a. Distributive property0
    b. Thing
    c. Undefined
    d. Undefined

77. _____ is change in population over time, and can be quantified as the change in the number of individuals in a population per unit time.
    a. Population growth0
    b. Thing
    c. Undefined
    d. Undefined

78. _____ are a measure of time.
    a. Thing
    b. Minutes0
    c. Undefined
    d. Undefined

79. In mathematics, there are several meanings of _____ depending on the subject.
    a. Thing
    b. Degree0
    c. Undefined
    d. Undefined

80. Acid _____ ratio measures the ability of a company to use its near cash or quick assets to immediately extinguish its current liabilities.
    a. Test0
    b. Thing
    c. Undefined
    d. Undefined

81. The deductive-nomological model is a formalized view of scientific _____ in natural language.
    a. Thing
    b. Explanation0
    c. Undefined
    d. Undefined

82. In mathematics, a _____ can mean either an element of the set {1, 2, 3, ...} (i.e the positive integers or the counting numbers) or an element of the set {0, 1, 2, 3, ...} (i.e. the non-negative integers).
    a. Natural number0
    b. Thing
    c. Undefined
    d. Undefined

83. In mathematics, an _____ is a statement about the relative size or order of two objects.
    a. Inequality0
    b. Thing
    c. Undefined
    d. Undefined

84. Two mathematical objects are equal if and only if they are precisely the same in every way. This defines a binary relation, _____, denoted by the sign of _____ "=" in such a way that the statement "x = y" means that x and y are equal.

Chapter 4. Linear Equations and inequalities in Two Variables

a. Equality0
b. Thing
c. Undefined
d. Undefined

85. In mathematics, _____ geometry was the traditional name for the geometry of three-dimensional Euclidean space — for practical purposes the kind of space we live in.
    a. Solid0
    b. Thing
    c. Undefined
    d. Undefined

86. An _____ is a straight line around which a geometric figure can be rotated.
    a. Thing
    b. Axis0
    c. Undefined
    d. Undefined

87. An _____ is the result from the sudden release of stored energy in the Earth's crust that creates seismic waves.
    a. Earthquake0
    b. Thing
    c. Undefined
    d. Undefined

88. The _____ of a solid object is the three-dimensional concept of how much space it occupies, often quantified numerically.
    a. Volume0
    b. Thing
    c. Undefined
    d. Undefined

89. _____ is the ability to hold, receive or absorb, or a measure thereof, similar to the concept of volume.
    a. Concept
    b. Capacity0
    c. Undefined
    d. Undefined

90. In mathematics and its applications, _____ are used for assigning an n-tuple of numbers or scalars to each point in an n-dimensional space.
    a. Coordinate systems0
    b. Concept
    c. Undefined
    d. Undefined

91. _____ are external two-dimensional outlines, with the appearance or configuration of some thing - in contrast to the matter or content or substance of which it is composed.
    a. Thing
    b. Shapes0
    c. Undefined
    d. Undefined

92. _____ is a notation for writing numbers that is often used by scientists and mathematicians to make it easier to write large and small numbers.
    a. Scientific notation0
    b. Thing
    c. Undefined
    d. Undefined

93. _____ is a temperature scale named after the German physicist Daniel Gabriel _____ , who proposed it in 1724.
    a. Fahrenheit0
    b. Thing
    c. Undefined
    d. Undefined

Chapter 4. Linear Equations and inequalities in Two Variables

94. In mathematics, an _____ number is any real number that is not a rational number- that is, it is a number which cannot be expressed as a fraction m/n, where m and n are integers.
    a. Thing
    b. Irrational0
    c. Undefined
    d. Undefined

95. In mathematics, an _____ is any real number that is not a rational number ¡ª that is, it is a number which cannot be expressed as m/n, where m and n are integers.
    a. Irrational number0
    b. Thing
    c. Undefined
    d. Undefined

96. In mathematics, _____ are any real number that is not a rational number ¡ª that is, it is a number which cannot be expressed as m/n, where m and n are integers.
    a. Thing
    b. Irrational numbers0
    c. Undefined
    d. Undefined

97. _____ is a unit of speed, expressing the number of international miles covered per hour.
    a. Thing
    b. Miles per hour0
    c. Undefined
    d. Undefined

98. A _____ is the part of the dividend that is left over when the dividend is not evenly divisible by the divisor.
    a. Remainder0
    b. Thing
    c. Undefined
    d. Undefined

99. _____ is the transport of people on a trip/journey or the process or time involved in a person or object moving from one location to another.
    a. Travel0
    b. Thing
    c. Undefined
    d. Undefined

100. In mathematics, the additive inverse, or _____ of a number n is the number that, when added to n, yields zero. The additive inverse of n is denoted −n. For example, 7 is −7, because 7 + (−7) = 0, and the additive inverse of −0.3 is 0.3, because −0.3 + 0.3 = 0.
    a. Thing
    b. Opposite0
    c. Undefined
    d. Undefined

101. In mathematics, the _____ of a number n is the number that, when added to n, yields zero. The _____ of n is denoted −n. For example, 7 is −7, because 7 + (−7) = 0, and the _____ of −0.3 is 0.3, because −0.3 + 0.3 = 0.
    a. Thing
    b. Additive inverse0
    c. Undefined
    d. Undefined

102. A _____ is one of the basic shapes of geometry: a polygon with three vertices and three sides which are straight line segments.
    a. Thing
    b. Triangle0
    c. Undefined
    d. Undefined

103. In mathematics, an inequality is a statement about the relative size or order of two objects. For example 14 > 10, or 14 is _____ 10.

a. Thing
c. Undefined
b. Greater than0
d. Undefined

104. _____ is a special mathematical relationship between two quantities. Two quantities are called proportional if they vary in such a way that one of the quantities is a constant multiple of the other, or equivalently if they have a constant ratio.
a. Proportionality0
c. Undefined
b. Thing
d. Undefined

Chapter 5. Systems of Linear Equations and Inequalities

1. In geometry, the _____ of an object is a point in some sense in the middle of the object.
   - a. Center0
   - b. Thing
   - c. Undefined
   - d. Undefined

2. A _____ is a symbolic representation denoting a quantity or expression. It often represents an "unknown" quantity that has the potential to change.
   - a. Variable0
   - b. Thing
   - c. Undefined
   - d. Undefined

3. In Graph theory, a _____ is a digraph with weighted edges.
   - a. Concept
   - b. Network0
   - c. Undefined
   - d. Undefined

4. In physics, _____ is an influence that may cause an object to accelerate. It may be experienced as a lift, a push, or a pull. The actual acceleration of the body is determined by the vector sum of all forces acting on it, known as net _____ or resultant _____.
   - a. Thing
   - b. Force0
   - c. Undefined
   - d. Undefined

5. An _____ is a collection of two not necessarily distinct objects, one of which is distinguished as the first coordinate and the other as the second coordinate.
   - a. Thing
   - b. Ordered pair0
   - c. Undefined
   - d. Undefined

6. The word _____ comes from the Latin word linearis, which means created by lines.
   - a. Linear0
   - b. Thing
   - c. Undefined
   - d. Undefined

7. A _____ is an equation in which each term is either a constant or the product of a constant times the first power of a variable.
   - a. Linear equation0
   - b. Thing
   - c. Undefined
   - d. Undefined

8. A _____ is a set of numbers that designate location in a given reference system, such as x,y in a planar _____ system or an x,y,z in a three-dimensional _____ system.
   - a. Coordinate0
   - b. Thing
   - c. Undefined
   - d. Undefined

9. In mathematics and its applications, a _____ is a system for assigning an n-tuple of numbers or scalars to each point in an n-dimensional space.
   - a. Concept
   - b. Coordinate system0
   - c. Undefined
   - d. Undefined

10. _____ are the basic objects of study in graph theory. Informally speaking, a graph is a set of objects called points, nodes, or vertices connected by links called lines or edges.

Chapter 5. Systems of Linear Equations and Inequalities

    a. Graphs0   b. Thing
    c. Undefined   d. Undefined

11. In mathematics, the _____ of two sets A and B is the set that contains all elements of A that also belong to B (or equivalently, all elements of B that also belong to A), but no other elements.
    a. Intersection0   b. Thing
    c. Undefined   d. Undefined

12. A _____ is a negotiable instrument instructing a financial institution to pay a specific amount of a specific currency from a specific demand account held in the maker/depositor's name with that institution. Both the maker and payee may be natural persons or legal entities.
    a. Check0   b. Thing
    c. Undefined   d. Undefined

13. In linear algebra, the _____ of an n-by-n square matrix A is defined to be the sum of the elements on the main diagonal of A,
    a. Trace0   b. Thing
    c. Undefined   d. Undefined

14. The _____ of measurement are a globally standardized and modernized form of the metric system.
    a. Units0   b. Thing
    c. Undefined   d. Undefined

15. _____ is often used to describe the measurement of the steepness, incline, gradient, or grade of a straight line. The _____ is defined as the ratio of the "rise" divided by the "run" between two points on a line, or in other words, the ratio of the altitude change to the horizontal distance between any two points on the line.
    a. Thing   b. Slope0
    c. Undefined   d. Undefined

16. The _____, the average in everyday English, which is also called the arithmetic _____ (and is distinguished from the geometric _____ or harmonic _____). The average is also called the sample _____. The expected value of a random variable, which is also called the population _____.
    a. Thing   b. Mean0
    c. Undefined   d. Undefined

17. The existence and properties of _____ are the basis of Euclid's parallel postulate. _____ are two lines on the same plane that do not intersect even assuming that lines extend to infinity in either direction.
    a. Thing   b. Parallel lines0
    c. Undefined   d. Undefined

18. Any point where a graph makes contact with an coordinate axis is called an _____ of the graph
    a. Intercept0   b. Thing
    c. Undefined   d. Undefined

19. _____ is the state of being greater than any finite real or natural number, however large.

Chapter 5. Systems of Linear Equations and Inequalities

a. Thing
b. Infinite0
c. Undefined
d. Undefined

20. A _____ is a quantity that denotes the proportional amount or magnitude of one quantity relative to another.
a. Ratio0
b. Thing
c. Undefined
d. Undefined

21. In plane geometry, a _____ is a polygon with four equal sides, four right angles, and parallel opposite sides. In algebra, the _____ of a number is that number multiplied by itself.
a. Square0
b. Thing
c. Undefined
d. Undefined

22. The word _____ is used in a variety of ways in mathematics.
a. Thing
b. Index0
c. Undefined
d. Undefined

23. A _____, scatter diagram or scatter graph is a chart that uses Cartesian coordinates to display values for two variables.
a. Thing
b. Scatter plot0
c. Undefined
d. Undefined

24. _____ is a synonym for information.
a. Thing
b. Data0
c. Undefined
d. Undefined

25. _____ is the level of functional and/or metabolic efficiency of an organism at both the micro level.
a. Thing
b. Health0
c. Undefined
d. Undefined

26. In astronomy, geography, geometry and related sciences and contexts, a plane is said to be _____ at a given point if it is locally perpendicular to the gradient of the gravity field, i.e., with the direction of the gravitational force at that point.
a. Horizontal0
b. Thing
c. Undefined
d. Undefined

27. _____ is a graph of the points representing a collection of data.
a. Thing
b. Scatter plots0
c. Undefined
d. Undefined

28. A _____ is a statement or claimt that a particular event will occur in the future in more certain terms than a forecast.
a. Prediction0
b. Thing
c. Undefined
d. Undefined

29. An _____ is when two lines intersect somewhere on a plane creating a right angle at intersection

Chapter 5. Systems of Linear Equations and Inequalities

a. Thing
b. Axes0
c. Undefined
d. Undefined

30. In geometry, a _____ is defined as a quadrilateral where all four of its angles are right angles.
a. Rectangle0
b. Thing
c. Undefined
d. Undefined

31. The _____ is used to discard one of the variables in an equation, only to replace it with the actual value when solving multiple equations.
a. Thing
b. Substitution method0
c. Undefined
d. Undefined

32. In economics, _____ describe market relations between prospective sellers and buyers of a good.
a. Thing
b. Supply and demand0
c. Undefined
d. Undefined

33. An _____ is a combination of numbers, operators, grouping symbols and/or free variables and bound variables arranged in a meaningful way which can be evaluated..
a. Thing
b. Expression0
c. Undefined
d. Undefined

34. In geographic information systems, a _____ comprises an entity with a geographic location, typically determined by points, arcs, or polygons. Carriageways and cadastres exemplify _____ data.
a. Feature0
b. Thing
c. Undefined
d. Undefined

35. In mathematics, a _____ is a constant multiplicative factor of a certain object. The object can be such things as a variable, a vector, a function, etc. For example, the _____ of $9x^2$ is 9.
a. Coefficient0
b. Thing
c. Undefined
d. Undefined

36. In common philosophical language, a proposition or _____, is the content of an assertion, that is, it is true-or-false and defined by the meaning of a particular piece of language.
a. Statement0
b. Concept
c. Undefined
d. Undefined

37. In mathematics, and in particular in abstract algebra, the _____ is a property of binary operations that generalises the distributive law from elementary algebra.
a. Distributive property0
b. Thing
c. Undefined
d. Undefined

38. _____ are a set of equations containing multiple variables.
a. Systems of equations0
b. Thing
c. Undefined
d. Undefined

39. In mathematics, a _____ is the result of multiplying, or an expression that identifies factors to be multiplied.

Chapter 5. Systems of Linear Equations and Inequalities 59

a. Thing
b. Product0
c. Undefined
d. Undefined

40. _____ is a mathematical science pertaining to the collection, analysis, interpretation or explanation, and presentation of data. It is applicable to a wide variety of academic disciplines, from the physical and social sciences to the humanities.
a. Thing
b. Statistics0
c. Undefined
d. Undefined

41. _____ studies and addresses the ways in which individuals, businesses, and organizations raise, allocate, and use monetary resources over time, taking into account the risks entailed in their projects
a. Finance0
b. Thing
c. Undefined
d. Undefined

42. A _____ is a special kind of ratio, indicating a relationship between two measurements with different units, such as miles to gallons or cents to pounds.
a. Thing
b. Rate0
c. Undefined
d. Undefined

43. _____, from Latin meaning "to make progress", is defined in two different ways. Pure economic _____ is the increase in wealth that an investor has from making an investment, taking into consideration all costs associated with that investment including the opportunity cost of capital.
a. Profit0
b. Thing
c. Undefined
d. Undefined

44. _____ is a business term for the amount of money that a company receives from its activities in a given period, mostly from sales of products and/or services to customers
a. Revenue0
b. Thing
c. Undefined
d. Undefined

45. U.S. liquid _____ is legally defined as 231 cubic inches, and is equal to 3.785411784 litres or abotu 0.13368 cubic feet. This is the most common definition of a _____. The U.S. fluid ounce is defined as 1/128 of a U.S. _____.
a. Thing
b. Gallon0
c. Undefined
d. Undefined

46. The deductive-nomological model is a formalized view of scientific _____ in natural language.
a. Thing
b. Explanation0
c. Undefined
d. Undefined

47. In economics, economic _____ is simply a state of the world where economic forces are balanced and in the absence of external influences the values of economic variables will not change.
a. Equilibrium0
b. Thing
c. Undefined
d. Undefined

48. _____ is the price at which the quantity demanded of a good or service is equal to the quantity supplied.

Chapter 5. Systems of Linear Equations and Inequalities

a. Equilibrium price0
b. Thing
c. Undefined
d. Undefined

49. A _____ is an individual or household that purchases and uses goods and services generated within the economy.
a. Consumer0
b. Thing
c. Undefined
d. Undefined

50. _____ is a kind of property which exists as magnitude or multitude. It is among the basic classes of things along with quality, substance, change, and relation.
a. Thing
b. Amount0
c. Undefined
d. Undefined

51. The _____ are the only integral domain whose positive elements are well-ordered, and in which order is preserved by addition. Like the natural numbers, the _____ form a countably infinite set. The set of all _____ is usually denoted in mathematics by a boldface Z .
a. Thing
b. Integers0
c. Undefined
d. Undefined

52. A _____ is the result of the addition of a set of numbers. The numbers may be natural numbers, complex numbers, matrices, or still more complicated objects. An infinite _____ is a subtle procedure known as a series.
a. Sum0
b. Thing
c. Undefined
d. Undefined

53. In mathematics, the additive inverse, or _____ of a number n is the number that, when added to n, yields zero. The additive inverse of n is denoted −n. For example, 7 is −7, because 7 + (−7) = 0, and the additive inverse of −0.3 is 0.3, because −0.3 + 0.3 = 0.
a. Thing
b. Opposite0
c. Undefined
d. Undefined

54. In mathematics and the mathematical sciences, a _____ is a fixed, but possibly unspecified, value. This is in contrast to a variable, which is not fixed.
a. Thing
b. Constant0
c. Undefined
d. Undefined

55. A _____ is 360° or 2δ radians.
a. Turn0
b. Thing
c. Undefined
d. Undefined

56. _____ or arithmetics is the oldest and most elementary branch of mathematics, used by almost everyone, for tasks ranging from simple daily counting to advanced science and business calculations.
a. Arithmetic0
b. Thing
c. Undefined
d. Undefined

57. _____ is a fixed, but possibly unspecified, value. This is in contrast to a variable, which is not fixed.

Chapter 5. Systems of Linear Equations and Inequalities

a. Thing
b. Constant term0
c. Undefined
d. Undefined

58. _____ forms part of thinking. Considered the most complex of all intellectual functions, _____ has been defined as higher-order cognitive process that requires the modulation and control of more routine or fundamental skills.
   a. Problem solving0
   b. Thing
   c. Undefined
   d. Undefined

59. In mathematics, a _____ is an n-tuple with n being 3.
   a. Triple0
   b. Thing
   c. Undefined
   d. Undefined

60. A _____ is a function that assigns a number to subsets of a given set.
   a. Measure0
   b. Thing
   c. Undefined
   d. Undefined

61. A _____ is a plan of action to guide decisions and actions.
   a. Policy0
   b. Thing
   c. Undefined
   d. Undefined

62. _____ is the distance around a given two-dimensional object. As a general rule, the _____ of a polygon can always be calculated by adding all the length of the sides together. So, the formula for triangles is P = a + b + c, where a, b and c stand for each side of it. For quadrilaterals the equation is P = a + b + c + d. For equilateral polygons, P = na, where n is the number of sides and a is the side length.
   a. Thing
   b. Perimeter0
   c. Undefined
   d. Undefined

63. A _____ is a large group of animals. The term is usually applied to mammals, particularly ungulates. Other terms are used for similar phenomena in other types of animal.
   a. Thing
   b. Herd0
   c. Undefined
   d. Undefined

64. In finance and economics, _____ is the process of finding the present value of an amount of cash at some future date, and along with compounding cash forms the basis of time value of money calculations.
   a. Thing
   b. Discount0
   c. Undefined
   d. Undefined

65. Equivalence is the condition of being _____ or essentially equal.
   a. Equivalent0
   b. Thing
   c. Undefined
   d. Undefined

66. _____ is the fee paid on borrowed money.
   a. Interest0
   b. Thing
   c. Undefined
   d. Undefined

67. _____ of a product is the price the manufacturer recommends that the retailer sell it for.

Chapter 5. Systems of Linear Equations and Inequalities

a. List price0
b. Thing
c. Undefined
d. Undefined

68. A _____ is a compensation which workers receive in exchange for their labor.
   a. Wage0
   b. Thing
   c. Undefined
   d. Undefined

69. _____ is a form of periodic payment from an employer to an employee, which is specified in an employment contract.
   a. Thing
   b. Gross pay0
   c. Undefined
   d. Undefined

70. In mathematics, an _____, mean, or central tendency of a data set refers to a measure of the "middle" or "expected" value of the data set.
   a. Average0
   b. Concept
   c. Undefined
   d. Undefined

71. A _____ is a form of periodic payment from an employer to an employee, which is specified in an employment contract.
   a. Thing
   b. Salary0
   c. Undefined
   d. Undefined

72. A _____ is one of the basic shapes of geometry: a polygon with three vertices and three sides which are straight line segments.
   a. Thing
   b. Triangle0
   c. Undefined
   d. Undefined

73. An _____ triange is a triangle with at least two sides of equal length.
   a. Isosceles0
   b. Thing
   c. Undefined
   d. Undefined

74. _____ is the transport of people on a trip/journey or the process or time involved in a person or object moving from one location to another.
   a. Thing
   b. Travel0
   c. Undefined
   d. Undefined

75. A _____ is a unit of length, usually used to measure distance, in a number of different systems, including Imperial units, United States customary units and Norwegian/Swedish mil. Its size can vary from system to system, but in each is between 1 and 10 kilometers. In contemporary English contexts _____ refers to either:
   a. Mile0
   b. Thing
   c. Undefined
   d. Undefined

76. In mathematics, a _____ is a two-dimensional manifold or surface that is perfectly flat.
   a. Plane0
   b. Thing
   c. Undefined
   d. Undefined

Chapter 5. Systems of Linear Equations and Inequalities

77. There are two main approaches to _____ in mathematics. They are the model theory of _____ and the proof theory of _____.
    a. Thing
    b. Truth0
    c. Undefined
    d. Undefined

78. The _____ of a ring R is defined to be the smallest positive integer n such that n a = 0, for all a in R.
    a. Characteristic0
    b. Thing
    c. Undefined
    d. Undefined

79. In mathematics, an _____ is a statement about the relative size or order of two objects.
    a. Thing
    b. Inequality0
    c. Undefined
    d. Undefined

80. A _____ is a set of possible values that a variable can take on in order to satisfy a given set of conditions, which may include equations and inequalities.
    a. Solution set0
    b. Thing
    c. Undefined
    d. Undefined

81. In mathematics, the conjugate _____ or adjoint matrix of an m-by-n matrix A with complex entries is the n-by-m matrix A* obtained from A by taking the transpose and then taking the complex conjugate of each entry.
    a. Thing
    b. Pairs0
    c. Undefined
    d. Undefined

82. Two mathematical objects are equal if and only if they are precisely the same in every way. This defines a binary relation, _____, denoted by the sign of _____ "=" in such a way that the statement "x = y" means that x and y are equal.
    a. Thing
    b. Equality0
    c. Undefined
    d. Undefined

83. In mathematics, _____ geometry was the traditional name for the geometry of three-dimensional Euclidean space — for practical purposes the kind of space we live in.
    a. Solid0
    b. Thing
    c. Undefined
    d. Undefined

84. A _____ consists of one quarter of the coordinate plane.
    a. Quadrant0
    b. Thing
    c. Undefined
    d. Undefined

85. In combinatorial mathematics, a _____ is an un-ordered collection of unique elements.
    a. Concept
    b. Combination0
    c. Undefined
    d. Undefined

86. _____ is the production of food, feed, fiber, fuel and other goods by the systematic raizing of plants and animals.
    a. Agriculture0
    b. Thing
    c. Undefined
    d. Undefined

Chapter 5. Systems of Linear Equations and Inequalities

87. In mathematics, the _____ of a function is the set of all "output" values produced by that function. Given a function $f : A \to B$, the _____ of f, is defined to be the set $\{x \in B : x = f(a) \text{ for some } a \in A\}$.
    a. Range0
    b. Thing
    c. Undefined
    d. Undefined

88. _____ or investing is a term with several closely-related meanings in business management, finance and economics, related to saving or deferring consumption.
    a. Investment0
    b. Thing
    c. Undefined
    d. Undefined

89. _____ are a measure of time.
    a. Thing
    b. Minutes0
    c. Undefined
    d. Undefined

90. The population _____ is the total number of human beings alive on the planet Earth at a given time.
    a. Thing
    b. Of the world0
    c. Undefined
    d. Undefined

91. A _____ is a one-dimensional picture in which the integers are shown as specially-marked points evenly spaced on a line.
    a. Number line0
    b. Thing
    c. Undefined
    d. Undefined

92. A _____ of a number is the product of that number with any integer.
    a. Thing
    b. Multiple0
    c. Undefined
    d. Undefined

93. In mathematics, a _____ can mean either an element of the set $\{1, 2, 3, \ldots\}$ (i.e the positive integers) or an element of the set $\{0, 1, 2, 3, \ldots\}$ (i.e. the non-negative integers).
    a. Concept
    b. Whole number0
    c. Undefined
    d. Undefined

94. In mathematics, a _____ is an expression that is constructed from one or more variables and constants, using only the operations of addition, subtraction, multiplication, and constant positive whole number exponents. is a _____. Note in particular that division by an expression containing a variable is not in general allowed in polynomials. [1]
    a. Thing
    b. Polynomial0
    c. Undefined
    d. Undefined

95. _____ has many meanings, most of which simply .
    a. Power0
    b. Thing
    c. Undefined
    d. Undefined

96. _____ is a branch of mathematics concerning the study of structure, relation and quantity.
    a. Algebra0
    b. Concept
    c. Undefined
    d. Undefined

Chapter 6. Exponents and Polynomials

1. A _____ is an abstract model that uses mathematical language to describe the behavior of a system. Eykhoff defined a _____ as 'a representation of the essential aspects of an existing system which presents knowledge of that system in usable form'.
   a. Thing
   b. Mathematical model0
   c. Undefined
   d. Undefined

2. In mathematics, a _____ is an expression that is constructed from one or more variables and constants, using only the operations of addition, subtraction, multiplication, and constant positive whole number exponents. is a _____. Note in particular that division by an expression containing a variable is not in general allowed in polynomials. [1]
   a. Polynomial0
   b. Thing
   c. Undefined
   d. Undefined

3. An _____ is a combination of numbers, operators, grouping symbols and/or free variables and bound variables arranged in a meaningful way which can be evaluated..
   a. Thing
   b. Expression0
   c. Undefined
   d. Undefined

4. A _____ is a symbolic representation denoting a quantity or expression. It often represents an "unknown" quantity that has the potential to change.
   a. Variable0
   b. Thing
   c. Undefined
   d. Undefined

5. A _____ is a numeral used to indicate a count. The most common use of the word today is to name the part of a fraction that tells the number or count of equal parts.
   a. Numerator0
   b. Thing
   c. Undefined
   d. Undefined

6. A _____ is the result of the addition of a set of numbers. The numbers may be natural numbers, complex numbers, matrices, or still more complicated objects. An infinite _____ is a subtle procedure known as a series.
   a. Thing
   b. Sum0
   c. Undefined
   d. Undefined

7. In mathematics, a _____ can mean either an element of the set {1, 2, 3, ...} (i.e the positive integers) or an element of the set {0, 1, 2, 3, ...} (i.e. the non-negative integers).
   a. Whole number0
   b. Concept
   c. Undefined
   d. Undefined

8. _____ is a mathematical operation, written a^n, involving two numbers, the base a and the exponent n.
   a. Thing
   b. Exponentiating0
   c. Undefined
   d. Undefined

9. _____ is a mathematical operation, written a^n, involving two numbers, the base a and the exponent n.
   a. Exponentiation0
   b. Thing
   c. Undefined
   d. Undefined

10. _____ has many meanings, most of which simply .

a. Power0
b. Thing
c. Undefined
d. Undefined

11. In mathematics, there are several meanings of _____ depending on the subject.
   a. Degree0
   b. Thing
   c. Undefined
   d. Undefined

12. In mathematics and the mathematical sciences, a _____ is a fixed, but possibly unspecified, value. This is in contrast to a variable, which is not fixed.
   a. Constant0
   b. Thing
   c. Undefined
   d. Undefined

13. In mathematics, a _____ is a particular kind of polynomial, having just one term.
   a. Thing
   b. Monomial0
   c. Undefined
   d. Undefined

14. In elementary algebra, a _____ is a polynomial with two terms: the sum of two monomials. It is the simplest kind of polynomial except for a monomial.
   a. Binomial0
   b. Thing
   c. Undefined
   d. Undefined

15. A _____ is a polynomial consisting of three terms; in other words, it is the sum of three monomials.
   a. Thing
   b. Trinomial0
   c. Undefined
   d. Undefined

16. The _____ is the maximum of the degrees of all terms in the polynomial.
   a. Thing
   b. Degree of a polynomial0
   c. Undefined
   d. Undefined

17. A _____ is a negotiable instrument instructing a financial institution to pay a specific amount of a specific currency from a specific demand account held in the maker/depositor's name with that institution. Both the maker and payee may be natural persons or legal entities.
   a. Check0
   b. Thing
   c. Undefined
   d. Undefined

18. In mathematics, a matrix can be thought of as each row or _____ being a vector. Hence, a space formed by row vectors or _____ vectors are said to be a row space or a _____ space.
   a. Concept
   b. Column0
   c. Undefined
   d. Undefined

19. In mathematics, a _____ may be described informally as a number that can be given by an infinite decimal representation.
   a. Thing
   b. Real number0
   c. Undefined
   d. Undefined

Chapter 6. Exponents and Polynomials

20. In mathematics, the additive inverse, or _____ of a number n is the number that, when added to n, yields zero. The additive inverse of n is denoted −n. For example, 7 is −7, because 7 + (−7) = 0, and the additive inverse of −0.3 is 0.3, because −0.3 + 0.3 = 0.
    a. Thing
    b. Opposite0
    c. Undefined
    d. Undefined

21. _____ element of an element x with respect to a binary operation * with identity element e is an element y such that x * y = y * x = e. In particular,
    a. Thing
    b. Inverse0
    c. Undefined
    d. Undefined

22. In mathematics, the _____ inverse, or opposite, of a number n is the number that, when added to n, yields zero. The _____ inverse of n is denoted −n.
    a. Additive0
    b. Thing
    c. Undefined
    d. Undefined

23. In mathematics, the _____ of a number n is the number that, when added to n, yields zero. The _____ of n is denoted −n. For example, 7 is −7, because 7 + (−7) = 0, and the _____ of −0.3 is 0.3, because −0.3 + 0.3 = 0.
    a. Additive inverse0
    b. Thing
    c. Undefined
    d. Undefined

24. _____ are the basic objects of study in graph theory. Informally speaking, a graph is a set of objects called points, nodes, or vertices connected by links called lines or edges.
    a. Thing
    b. Graphs0
    c. Undefined
    d. Undefined

25. Equivalence is the condition of being _____ or essentially equal.
    a. Equivalent0
    b. Thing
    c. Undefined
    d. Undefined

26. _____ is a set, with some particular properties and usually some additional structure, such as the operations of addition or multiplication, for instance.
    a. Thing
    b. Space0
    c. Undefined
    d. Undefined

27. A _____ is a compensation which workers receive in exchange for their labor.
    a. Thing
    b. Wage0
    c. Undefined
    d. Undefined

28. _____ (Groups, Algorithms and Programming) is a computer algebra system for computational discrete algebra with particular emphasis on, but not restricted to, computational group theory.
    a. Thing
    b. Gap0
    c. Undefined
    d. Undefined

29. In mathematics, an _____, mean, or central tendency of a data set refers to a measure of the "middle" or "expected" value of the data set.

Chapter 6. Exponents and Polynomials

    a. Average0
    b. Concept
    c. Undefined
    d. Undefined

30. _____ is a way of expressing a number as a fraction of 100 per cent meaning "per hundred".
    a. Percent0
    b. Thing
    c. Undefined
    d. Undefined

31. _____ is a synonym for information.
    a. Data0
    b. Thing
    c. Undefined
    d. Undefined

32. In mathematics, a _____ is a constant multiplicative factor of a certain object. The object can be such things as a variable, a vector, a function, etc. For example, the _____ of $9x^2$ is 9.
    a. Coefficient0
    b. Thing
    c. Undefined
    d. Undefined

33. _____ is a notation for writing numbers that is often used by scientists and mathematicians to make it easier to write large and small numbers.
    a. Scientific notation0
    b. Thing
    c. Undefined
    d. Undefined

34. A _____ is a plan of action to guide decisions and actions.
    a. Thing
    b. Policy0
    c. Undefined
    d. Undefined

35. In mathematics, a _____ is the result of multiplying, or an expression that identifies factors to be multiplied.
    a. Thing
    b. Product0
    c. Undefined
    d. Undefined

36. The _____ governs the differentiation of products of differentiable functions.
    a. Thing
    b. Product rule0
    c. Undefined
    d. Undefined

37. In mathematics, _____ growth occurs when the growth rate of a function is always proportional to the function's current size.
    a. Thing
    b. Exponential0
    c. Undefined
    d. Undefined

38. In mathematics, factorization (British English: factorisation) or factoring is the decomposition of an object (for example, a number, a polynomial, or a matrix) into a product of other objects, or _____, which when multiplied together give the original.
    a. Factors0
    b. Thing
    c. Undefined
    d. Undefined

39. _____, either of the curved-bracket punctuation marks that together make a set of _____

Chapter 6. Exponents and Polynomials

a. Parentheses0
c. Undefined
b. Thing
d. Undefined

40. _____ is a method for differentiating expressions involving exponentiation the power operation.
   a. Thing
   b. Power rule0
   c. Undefined
   d. Undefined

41. A _____ is a three-dimensional solid object bounded by six square faces, facets, or sides, with three meeting at each vertex.
   a. Cube0
   b. Thing
   c. Undefined
   d. Undefined

42. In mathematics, and in particular in abstract algebra, the _____ is a property of binary operations that generalises the distributive law from elementary algebra.
   a. Distributive property0
   b. Thing
   c. Undefined
   d. Undefined

43. In mathematics, _____ is an elementary arithmetic operation. When one of the numbers is a whole number, _____ is the repeated sum of the other number.
   a. Thing
   b. Multiplication0
   c. Undefined
   d. Undefined

44. In geometry, a _____ is defined as a quadrilateral where all four of its angles are right angles.
   a. Thing
   b. Rectangle0
   c. Undefined
   d. Undefined

45. In a mathematical proof or a syllogism, a _____ is a statement that is the logical consequence of preceding statements.
   a. Conclusion0
   b. Concept
   c. Undefined
   d. Undefined

46. _____ is a physical property of a system that underlies the common notions of hot and cold; something that is hotter has the greater _____.
   a. Thing
   b. Temperature0
   c. Undefined
   d. Undefined

47. A _____, as defined by the International Astronomical Union, is a celestial body orbiting a star or stellar remnant that is massive enough to be rounded by its own gravity, not massive enough to cause thermonuclear fusion in its core, and has cleared its neighboring region of planetesimals.
   a. Thing
   b. Planet0
   c. Undefined
   d. Undefined

48. A _____ is a special kind of ratio, indicating a relationship between two measurements with different units, such as miles to gallons or cents to pounds.

Chapter 6. Exponents and Polynomials

    a. Thing
    b. Rate0
    c. Undefined
    d. Undefined

49. In mathematics, the concept of a _____ tries to capture the intuitive idea of a geometrical one-dimensional and continuous object. A simple example is the circle.
    a. Thing
    b. Curve0
    c. Undefined
    d. Undefined

50. In astronomy, geography, geometry and related sciences and contexts, a plane is said to be _____ at a given point if it is locally perpendicular to the gradient of the gravity field, i.e., with the direction of the gravitational force at that point.
    a. Thing
    b. Horizontal0
    c. Undefined
    d. Undefined

51. Any point where a graph makes contact with an coordinate axis is called an _____ of the graph
    a. Intercept0
    b. Thing
    c. Undefined
    d. Undefined

52. _____ is often used to describe the measurement of the steepness, incline, gradient, or grade of a straight line. The _____ is defined as the ratio of the "rise" divided by the "run" between two points on a line, or in other words, the ratio of the altitude change to the horizontal distance between any two points on the line.
    a. Slope0
    b. Thing
    c. Undefined
    d. Undefined

53. _____ also sometimes known as the double distributive property or more colloquially as foiling, is commonly taught to US high school students learning algebra as a mnemonic for remembering how to multiply two binomials polynomials with two terms.
    a. FOIL method0
    b. Thing
    c. Undefined
    d. Undefined

54. The _____ is commonly taught to US high school students learning algebra as a mnemonic for remembering how to multiply two binomials.
    a. FOIL rule0
    b. Thing
    c. Undefined
    d. Undefined

55. In plane geometry, a _____ is a polygon with four equal sides, four right angles, and parallel opposite sides. In algebra, the _____ of a number is that number multiplied by itself.
    a. Square0
    b. Thing
    c. Undefined
    d. Undefined

56. The plus and _____ signs are mathematical symbols used to represent the notions of positive and negative as well as the operations of addition and subtraction.
    a. Thing
    b. Minus0
    c. Undefined
    d. Undefined

57. In mathematics, _____ expressions is used to reduce the expression into the lowest possible term.

Chapter 6. Exponents and Polynomials

    a. Simplifying0   b. Thing
    c. Undefined   d. Undefined

58. _____ is a branch of mathematics concerning the study of structure, relation and quantity.
    a. Concept   b. Algebra0
    c. Undefined   d. Undefined

59. A _____ is a function that assigns a number to subsets of a given set.
    a. Measure0   b. Thing
    c. Undefined   d. Undefined

60. In geometry, _____ angles are angles that have a common ray coming out of the vertex going between two other rays.
    a. Concept   b. Adjacent0
    c. Undefined   d. Undefined

61. The _____ of a solid object is the three-dimensional concept of how much space it occupies, often quantified numerically.
    a. Volume0   b. Thing
    c. Undefined   d. Undefined

62. In mathematics, a _____ is a two-dimensional manifold or surface that is perfectly flat.
    a. Thing   b. Plane0
    c. Undefined   d. Undefined

63. A _____ (or shape) refers to the external two-dimensional outline, appearance or configuration of some thing - in contrast to the matter or content or substance of which it is composed.
    a. Thing   b. Plane figure0
    c. Undefined   d. Undefined

64. In geometry, a _____ (Greek words diairo = divide and metro = measure) of a circle is any straight line segment that passes through the centre and whose endpoints are on the circular boundary, or, in more modern usage, the length of such a line segment. When using the word in the more modern sense, one speaks of the _____ rather than a _____, because all diameters of a circle have the same length. This length is twice the radius. The _____ of a circle is also the longest chord that the circle has.
    a. Diameter0   b. Thing
    c. Undefined   d. Undefined

65. Compass and straightedge or ruler-and-compass _____ is the _____ of lengths or angles using only an idealized ruler and compass.
    a. Thing   b. Construction0
    c. Undefined   d. Undefined

66. In geometry, the _____ of an object is a point in some sense in the middle of the object.

Chapter 6. Exponents and Polynomials

a. Thing
b. Center0
c. Undefined
d. Undefined

67. In arithmetic and algebra, when a number or expression is both preceded and followed by a binary operation, an _____ is required for which operation should be applied first.
   a. Order of operations0
   b. Thing
   c. Undefined
   d. Undefined

68. _____ is the act of putting ones into groups of 10.
   a. Regrouping0
   b. Thing
   c. Undefined
   d. Undefined

69. _____ of an object is its speed in a particular direction.
   a. Velocity0
   b. Thing
   c. Undefined
   d. Undefined

70. An _____ is a straight line around which a geometric figure can be rotated.
   a. Thing
   b. Axis0
   c. Undefined
   d. Undefined

71. _____ is a special mathematical relationship between two quantities. Two quantities are called proportional if they vary in such a way that one of the quantities is a constant multiple of the other, or equivalently if they have a constant ratio.
   a. Proportionality0
   b. Thing
   c. Undefined
   d. Undefined

72. In mathematics, a _____ is the end result of a division problem. It can also be expressed as the number of times the divisor divides into the dividend.
   a. Thing
   b. Quotient0
   c. Undefined
   d. Undefined

73. The _____ is a method of finding the derivative of a function that is the quotient of two other functions for which derivatives exist.
   a. Thing
   b. Quotient rule0
   c. Undefined
   d. Undefined

74. _____ is the level of functional and/or metabolic efficiency of an organism at both the micro level.
   a. Health0
   b. Thing
   c. Undefined
   d. Undefined

75. The _____, the average in everyday English, which is also called the arithmetic _____ (and is distinguished from the geometric _____ or harmonic _____). The average is also called the sample _____. The expected value of a random variable, which is also called the population _____.
   a. Thing
   b. Mean0
   c. Undefined
   d. Undefined

Chapter 6. Exponents and Polynomials 73

76. A _____ is the part of a fraction that tells how many equal parts make up a whole, and which is used in the name of the fraction: "halves", "thirds", "fourths" or "quarters", "fifths" and so on.
   a. Concept
   b. Denominator0
   c. Undefined
   d. Undefined

77. A _____ is 360° or 2δ radians.
   a. Thing
   b. Turn0
   c. Undefined
   d. Undefined

78. _____ is a payment made by a company to its shareholders
   a. Thing
   b. Dividend0
   c. Undefined
   d. Undefined

79. In mathematics, a _____ of an integer n, also called a factor of n, is an integer which evenly divides n without leaving a remainder.
   a. Divisor0
   b. Thing
   c. Undefined
   d. Undefined

80. In mathematics, the _____ (or modulus) of a real number is its numerical value without regard to its sign.
   a. Thing
   b. Absolute value0
   c. Undefined
   d. Undefined

81. In arithmetic, _____ is a procedure for calculating the division of one integer, called the dividend, by another integer called the divisor, to produce a result called the quotient.
   a. Thing
   b. Long division0
   c. Undefined
   d. Undefined

82. A _____ is the part of the dividend that is left over when the dividend is not evenly divisible by the divisor.
   a. Remainder0
   b. Thing
   c. Undefined
   d. Undefined

83. A _____ is a unit of length, usually used to measure distance, in a number of different systems, including Imperial units, United States customary units and Norwegian/Swedish mil. Its size can vary from system to system, but in each is between 1 and 10 kilometers. In contemporary English contexts _____ refers to either:
   a. Mile0
   b. Thing
   c. Undefined
   d. Undefined

84. _____ is a unit of speed, expressing the number of international miles covered per hour.
   a. Miles per hour0
   b. Thing
   c. Undefined
   d. Undefined

85. A _____ is a quantity that denotes the proportional amount or magnitude of one quantity relative to another.
   a. Thing
   b. Ratio0
   c. Undefined
   d. Undefined

86. Mathematical _____ is used to represent ideas.

Chapter 6. Exponents and Polynomials

a. Thing
c. Undefined
b. Notation0
d. Undefined

87. _____ is the writing of numbers in the base-ten numeral system, which uses various symbols called digits for ten distinct values 0, 1, 2, 3, 4, 5, 6, 7, 8 and 9 to represent numbers
    a. Thing
    c. Undefined
    b. Decimal notation0
    d. Undefined

88. In mathematics, a _____ can mean either an element of the set {1, 2, 3, ...} (i.e the positive integers or the counting numbers) or an element of the set {0, 1, 2, 3, ...} (i.e. the non-negative integers).
    a. Natural number0
    c. Undefined
    b. Thing
    d. Undefined

89. A _____ is a number that is less than zero.
    a. Negative number0
    c. Undefined
    b. Thing
    d. Undefined

90. In mathematics, an inequality is a statement about the relative size or order of two objects. For example 14 > 10, or 14 is _____ 10.
    a. Thing
    c. Undefined
    b. Greater than0
    d. Undefined

91. The decimal separator is a symbol used to mark the boundary between the integral and the fractional parts of a decimal numeral. Terms implying the symbol used are _____ and decimal comma.
    a. Decimal point0
    c. Undefined
    b. Concept
    d. Undefined

92. _____ studies and addresses the ways in which individuals, businesses, and organizations raise, allocate, and use monetary resources over time, taking into account the risks entailed in their projects
    a. Thing
    c. Undefined
    b. Finance0
    d. Undefined

93. _____ is a kind of property which exists as magnitude or multitude. It is among the basic classes of things along with quality, substance, change, and relation.
    a. Thing
    c. Undefined
    b. Amount0
    d. Undefined

94. In Euclidean geometry, a uniform _____ is a linear transformation that enlargers or diminishes objects, and whose _____ factor is the same in all directions. This is also called homothethy.
    a. Scale0
    c. Undefined
    b. Thing
    d. Undefined

95. The _____ of a mathematical object is its size: a property by which it can be larger or smaller than other objects of the same kind; in technical terms, an ordering of the class of objects to which it belongs.

Chapter 6. Exponents and Polynomials

a. Thing
c. Undefined
b. Magnitude0
d. Undefined

96. An _____ is the result from the sudden release of stored energy in the Earth's crust that creates seismic waves.
a. Thing
c. Undefined
b. Earthquake0
d. Undefined

97. In common philosophical language, a proposition or _____, is the content of an assertion, that is, it is true-or-false and defined by the meaning of a particular piece of language.
a. Statement0
c. Undefined
b. Concept
d. Undefined

98. Multiple Signal Classification, also known as _____, is an algorithm used for frequency estimation and emitter location.
a. Thing
c. Undefined
b. Music0
d. Undefined

99. The metre (or _____, see spelling differences) is a measure of length. It is the basic unit of length in the metric system and in the International System of Units (SI), used around the world for general and scientific purposes.
a. Meter0
c. Undefined
b. Concept
d. Undefined

100. A _____ is an individual or household that purchases and uses goods and services generated within the economy.
a. Consumer0
c. Undefined
b. Thing
d. Undefined

101. _____ primarily refers to social welfare service concerned with social protection, or protection against socially recognized conditions, including poverty, old age, disability, unemployment, families with children and others.
a. Social security0
c. Undefined
b. Thing
d. Undefined

102. Transport or _____ is the movement of people and goods from one place to another.
a. Transportation0
c. Undefined
b. Thing
d. Undefined

103. _____ is the fee paid on borrowed money.
a. Thing
c. Undefined
b. Interest0
d. Undefined

104. _____ is the production of food, feed, fiber, fuel and other goods by the systematic raizing of plants and animals.
a. Agriculture0
c. Undefined
b. Thing
d. Undefined

105. In sociology and biology a _____ is the collection of people or organisms of a particular species living in a given geographic area or space, usually measured by a census.

a. Thing
b. Population0
c. Undefined
d. Undefined

106. In statistics, _____ means the most frequent value assumed by a random variable, or occurring in a sampling of a random variable.
a. Concept
b. Mode0
c. Undefined
d. Undefined

107. _____ is a subset of a population.
a. Thing
b. Sample0
c. Undefined
d. Undefined

108. The _____ is the sum of the exponents of the variables in the term.
a. Thing
b. Degree of a term0
c. Undefined
d. Undefined

109. In mathematics, a _____ is any one of several different types of functions, mappings, operations, or transformations.
a. Projection0
b. Thing
c. Undefined
d. Undefined

110. A _____ is a one-dimensional picture in which the integers are shown as specially-marked points evenly spaced on a line.
a. Number line0
b. Thing
c. Undefined
d. Undefined

111. A _____ is a set of possible values that a variable can take on in order to satisfy a given set of conditions, which may include equations and inequalities.
a. Solution set0
b. Thing
c. Undefined
d. Undefined

Chapter 7. Factoring Polynomials

1. In mathematics, the _____ divisor of two non-zero integers, is the largest positive integer that divides both numbers without remainder.
   a. Thing
   b. Greatest common0
   c. Undefined
   d. Undefined

2. In Math the greates common divisor sometimes known as the _____ of two non- zero integers.
   a. Greatest common factor0
   b. Thing
   c. Undefined
   d. Undefined

3. _____ is the largest positive integer that divides both numbers without remainder.
   a. Thing
   b. Common Factor0
   c. Undefined
   d. Undefined

4. In mathematics, a _____ is an expression that is constructed from one or more variables and constants, using only the operations of addition, subtraction, multiplication, and constant positive whole number exponents. is a _____. Note in particular that division by an expression containing a variable is not in general allowed in polynomials. [1]
   a. Polynomial0
   b. Thing
   c. Undefined
   d. Undefined

5. _____ is a branch of mathematics concerning the study of structure, relation and quantity.
   a. Concept
   b. Algebra0
   c. Undefined
   d. Undefined

6. In mathematics, a _____ number (or a _____) is a natural number that has exactly two (distinct) natural number divisors, which are 1 and the _____ number itself.
   a. Thing
   b. Prime0
   c. Undefined
   d. Undefined

7. In mathematics, a _____ is a constant multiplicative factor of a certain object. The object can be such things as a variable, a vector, a function, etc. For example, the _____ of $9x^2$ is 9.
   a. Coefficient0
   b. Thing
   c. Undefined
   d. Undefined

8. The _____ are the only integral domain whose positive elements are well-ordered, and in which order is preserved by addition. Like the natural numbers, the _____ form a countably infinite set. The set of all _____ is usually denoted in mathematics by a boldface Z .
   a. Integers0
   b. Thing
   c. Undefined
   d. Undefined

9. In mathematics, a _____ is a particular kind of polynomial, having just one term.
   a. Monomial0
   b. Thing
   c. Undefined
   d. Undefined

10. In mathematics, a _____ is the result of multiplying, or an expression that identifies factors to be multiplied.
    a. Thing
    b. Product0
    c. Undefined
    d. Undefined

Chapter 7. Factoring Polynomials

11. In mathematics, _____ is the decomposition of an object into a product of other objects, or factors, which when multiplied together give the original.
    a. Factoring0
    b. Thing
    c. Undefined
    d. Undefined

12. The _____, the average in everyday English, which is also called the arithmetic _____ (and is distinguished from the geometric _____ or harmonic _____). The average is also called the sample _____. The expected value of a random variable, which is also called the population _____.
    a. Thing
    b. Mean0
    c. Undefined
    d. Undefined

13. In mathematics, and in particular in abstract algebra, the _____ is a property of binary operations that generalises the distributive law from elementary algebra.
    a. Distributive property0
    b. Thing
    c. Undefined
    d. Undefined

14. In elementary algebra, a _____ is a polynomial with two terms: the sum of two monomials. It is the simplest kind of polynomial except for a monomial.
    a. Binomial0
    b. Thing
    c. Undefined
    d. Undefined

15. In mathematics, the _____ of two non-zero integers, is the largest positive integer that divides both numbers without remainder.
    a. Greatest common divisor0
    b. Thing
    c. Undefined
    d. Undefined

16. An _____ is a combination of numbers, operators, grouping symbols and/or free variables and bound variables arranged in a meaningful way which can be evaluated..
    a. Expression0
    b. Thing
    c. Undefined
    d. Undefined

17. In mathematics, there are several meanings of _____ depending on the subject.
    a. Degree0
    b. Thing
    c. Undefined
    d. Undefined

18. A _____ is a symbolic representation denoting a quantity or expression. It often represents an "unknown" quantity that has the potential to change.
    a. Thing
    b. Variable0
    c. Undefined
    d. Undefined

19. _____ has many meanings, most of which simply .
    a. Power0
    b. Thing
    c. Undefined
    d. Undefined

20. A _____ is the result of the addition of a set of numbers. The numbers may be natural numbers, complex numbers, matrices, or still more complicated objects. An infinite _____ is a subtle procedure known as a series.

Chapter 7. Factoring Polynomials

a. Thing
b. Sum0
c. Undefined
d. Undefined

21. In mathematics, factorization (British English: factorisation) or factoring is the decomposition of an object (for example, a number, a polynomial, or a matrix) into a product of other objects, or _____, which when multiplied together give the original.
   a. Factors0
   b. Thing
   c. Undefined
   d. Undefined

22. _____ was a French lawyer and a mathematician who is given credit for early developments that led to modern calculus. In particular, he is recognized for his discovery of an original method of finding the greatest and the smallest ordinates of curved lines, which is analogous to that of the then unknown differential calculus.
   a. Pierre de Fermat0
   b. Person
   c. Undefined
   d. Undefined

23. In mathematics, the conjugate _____ or adjoint matrix of an m-by-n matrix A with complex entries is the n-by-m matrix A* obtained from A by taking the transpose and then taking the complex conjugate of each entry.
   a. Pairs0
   b. Thing
   c. Undefined
   d. Undefined

24. In mathematics, _____ is an elementary arithmetic operation. When one of the numbers is a whole number, _____ is the repeated sum of the other number.
   a. Multiplication0
   b. Thing
   c. Undefined
   d. Undefined

25. A _____ is a negotiable instrument instructing a financial institution to pay a specific amount of a specific currency from a specific demand account held in the maker/depositor's name with that institution. Both the maker and payee may be natural persons or legal entities.
   a. Thing
   b. Check0
   c. Undefined
   d. Undefined

26. _____ the expected value of a random variable displays the average or central value of the variable.It is a summary value of the distribution of the variable.
   a. Determining0
   b. Thing
   c. Undefined
   d. Undefined

27. In abstract algebra, _____ consists of sets with binary operations that satisfy certain axioms.
   a. Thing
   b. Grouping0
   c. Undefined
   d. Undefined

28. _____ is a mathematical operation, written a^n, involving two numbers, the base a and the exponent n.
   a. Thing
   b. Exponentiating0
   c. Undefined
   d. Undefined

29. _____ is a mathematical operation, written a^n, involving two numbers, the base a and the exponent n.

a. Exponentiation0
b. Thing
c. Undefined
d. Undefined

30. _____ also sometimes known as the double distributive property or more colloquially as foiling, is commonly taught to US high school students learning algebra as a mnemonic for remembering how to multiply two binomials polynomials with two terms.
   a. FOIL method0
   b. Thing
   c. Undefined
   d. Undefined

31. The _____ is commonly taught to US high school students learning algebra as a mnemonic for remembering how to multiply two binomials.
   a. Thing
   b. FOIL rule0
   c. Undefined
   d. Undefined

32. A _____ is a number that is less than zero.
   a. Negative number0
   b. Thing
   c. Undefined
   d. Undefined

33. The _____ is a property of multiplication or addition where the product or sum remains the same, regardless of whether or not the order of the addends or factors are changed.
   a. Commutative property0
   b. Thing
   c. Undefined
   d. Undefined

34. _____ of an object is its speed in a particular direction.
   a. Thing
   b. Velocity0
   c. Undefined
   d. Undefined

35. Initial objects are also called _____, and terminal objects are also called final.
   a. Coterminal0
   b. Thing
   c. Undefined
   d. Undefined

36. A _____ is a vehicle, missile or aircraft which obtains thrust by the reaction to the ejection of fast moving fluid from within a _____ engine.
   a. Rocket0
   b. Thing
   c. Undefined
   d. Undefined

37. In geometry, a _____ is defined as a quadrilateral where all four of its angles are right angles.
   a. Rectangle0
   b. Thing
   c. Undefined
   d. Undefined

38. A _____ is a polynomial consisting of three terms; in other words, it is the sum of three monomials.
   a. Thing
   b. Trinomial0
   c. Undefined
   d. Undefined

39. _____ are the basic objects of study in graph theory. Informally speaking, a graph is a set of objects called points, nodes, or vertices connected by links called lines or edges.

Chapter 7. Factoring Polynomials

a. Thing
c. Undefined
b. Graphs0
d. Undefined

40. In mathematics and the mathematical sciences, a _____ is a fixed, but possibly unspecified, value. This is in contrast to a variable, which is not fixed.
    a. Thing
    c. Undefined
    b. Constant0
    d. Undefined

41. In combinatorial mathematics, a _____ is an un-ordered collection of unique elements.
    a. Concept
    c. Undefined
    b. Combination0
    d. Undefined

42. The _____ of a solid object is the three-dimensional concept of how much space it occupies, often quantified numerically.
    a. Volume0
    c. Undefined
    b. Thing
    d. Undefined

43. In plane geometry, a _____ is a polygon with four equal sides, four right angles, and parallel opposite sides. In algebra, the _____ of a number is that number multiplied by itself.
    a. Square0
    c. Undefined
    b. Thing
    d. Undefined

44. In set theory and other branches of mathematics, the _____ of a collection of sets is the set that contains everything that belongs to any of the sets, but nothing else.
    a. Union0
    c. Undefined
    b. Thing
    d. Undefined

45. In mathematics the _____ refers to the identity: $a^2 - b^2 = (a+b)(a-b)$
    a. Thing
    c. Undefined
    b. Difference of two squares0
    d. Undefined

46. _____ forms part of thinking. Considered the most complex of all intellectual functions, _____ has been defined as higher-order cognitive process that requires the modulation and control of more routine or fundamental skills.
    a. Thing
    c. Undefined
    b. Problem solving0
    d. Undefined

47. In mathematics, a _____ may be described informally as a number that can be given by an infinite decimal representation.
    a. Thing
    c. Undefined
    b. Real number0
    d. Undefined

48. The term _____ can refer to an integer which is the square of some other integer, or an algebraic expression that can be factored as the square of some other expression.
    a. Thing
    c. Undefined
    b. Perfect square0
    d. Undefined

49. In a mathematical proof or a syllogism, a _____ is a statement that is the logical consequence of preceding statements.
   a. Concept
   b. Conclusion0
   c. Undefined
   d. Undefined

50. A _____ is a three-dimensional solid object bounded by six square faces, facets, or sides, with three meeting at each vertex.
   a. Cube0
   b. Thing
   c. Undefined
   d. Undefined

51. _____ are of a number n in its third power-the result of multiplying it by itself three times.
   a. Thing
   b. Cubes0
   c. Undefined
   d. Undefined

52. In mathematics, the additive inverse, or _____ of a number n is the number that, when added to n, yields zero. The additive inverse of n is denoted −n. For example, 7 is −7, because 7 + (−7) = 0, and the additive inverse of −0.3 is 0.3, because −0.3 + 0.3 = 0.
   a. Thing
   b. Opposite0
   c. Undefined
   d. Undefined

53. In mathematics, the _____ of a number n is the number that, when added to n, yields zero. The _____ of n is denoted −n. For example, 7 is −7, because 7 + (−7) = 0, and the _____ of −0.3 is 0.3, because −0.3 + 0.3 = 0.
   a. Thing
   b. Additive inverse0
   c. Undefined
   d. Undefined

54. In mathematics, an inequality is a statement about the relative size or order of two objects. For example 14 > 10, or 14 is _____ 10.
   a. Thing
   b. Greater than0
   c. Undefined
   d. Undefined

55. In mathematics, a _____ is an algebraic structure in which addition and multiplication are defined and have properties listed below.
   a. Thing
   b. Ring0
   c. Undefined
   d. Undefined

56. In sociology and biology a _____ is the collection of people or organisms of a particular species living in a given geographic area or space, usually measured by a census.
   a. Thing
   b. Population0
   c. Undefined
   d. Undefined

57. In common philosophical language, a proposition or _____, is the content of an assertion, that is, it is true-or-false and defined by the meaning of a particular piece of language.
   a. Statement0
   b. Concept
   c. Undefined
   d. Undefined

58. In mathematics, a _____ is a polynomial equation of the second degree. The general form is $ax^2 + bx + c = 0$.

Chapter 7. Factoring Polynomials

    a. Thing
    b. Quadratic equation0
    c. Undefined
    d. Undefined

59. _____ is a notation for writing numbers that is often used by scientists and mathematicians to make it easier to write large and small numbers.
    a. Scientific notation0
    b. Thing
    c. Undefined
    d. Undefined

60. A _____ signifies a point or points of probability on a subject e.g., the _____ of creativity, which allows for the formation of rule or norm or law by interpretation of the phenomena events that can be created.
    a. Principle0
    b. Thing
    c. Undefined
    d. Undefined

61. The word _____ comes from the Latin word linearis, which means created by lines.
    a. Thing
    b. Linear0
    c. Undefined
    d. Undefined

62. A _____ is an equation in which each term is either a constant or the product of a constant times the first power of a variable.
    a. Linear equation0
    b. Thing
    c. Undefined
    d. Undefined

63. A _____ is an abstract model that uses mathematical language to describe the behavior of a system. Eykhoff defined a _____ as 'a representation of the essential aspects of an existing system which presents knowledge of that system in usable form'.
    a. Mathematical model0
    b. Thing
    c. Undefined
    d. Undefined

64. An _____ is a straight line around which a geometric figure can be rotated.
    a. Axis0
    b. Thing
    c. Undefined
    d. Undefined

65. In astronomy, geography, geometry and related sciences and contexts, a plane is said to be _____ at a given point if it is locally perpendicular to the gradient of the gravity field, i.e., with the direction of the gravitational force at that point.
    a. Thing
    b. Horizontal0
    c. Undefined
    d. Undefined

66. A _____ consists of one quarter of the coordinate plane.
    a. Quadrant0
    b. Thing
    c. Undefined
    d. Undefined

67. The metre (or _____, see spelling differences) is a measure of length. It is the basic unit of length in the metric system and in the International System of Units (SI), used around the world for general and scientific purposes.
    a. Concept
    b. Meter0
    c. Undefined
    d. Undefined

Chapter 7. Factoring Polynomials

68. A _____ is one of the basic shapes of geometry: a polygon with three vertices and three sides which are straight line segments.
   a. Thing
   b. Triangle0
   c. Undefined
   d. Undefined

69. The plus and _____ signs are mathematical symbols used to represent the notions of positive and negative as well as the operations of addition and subtraction.
   a. Minus0
   b. Thing
   c. Undefined
   d. Undefined

70. In geographic information systems, a _____ comprises an entity with a geographic location, typically determined by points, arcs, or polygons. Carriageways and cadastres exemplify _____ data.
   a. Thing
   b. Feature0
   c. Undefined
   d. Undefined

71. In mathematics, a _____ can mean either an element of the set {1, 2, 3, ...} (i.e the positive integers) or an element of the set {0, 1, 2, 3, ...} (i.e. the non-negative integers).
   a. Whole number0
   b. Concept
   c. Undefined
   d. Undefined

72. _____ is a parameter associated with every conic section.
   a. Thing
   b. Eccentricity0
   c. Undefined
   d. Undefined

73. _____ is a set, with some particular properties and usually some additional structure, such as the operations of addition or multiplication, for instance.
   a. Thing
   b. Space0
   c. Undefined
   d. Undefined

74. Mathematical _____ is used to represent ideas.
   a. Thing
   b. Notation0
   c. Undefined
   d. Undefined

75. A _____ is a set of possible values that a variable can take on in order to satisfy a given set of conditions, which may include equations and inequalities.
   a. Solution set0
   b. Thing
   c. Undefined
   d. Undefined

76. A _____ is a function that assigns a number to subsets of a given set.
   a. Thing
   b. Measure0
   c. Undefined
   d. Undefined

77. _____ is often used to describe the measurement of the steepness, incline, gradient, or grade of a straight line. The _____ is defined as the ratio of the "rise" divided by the "run" between two points on a line, or in other words, the ratio of the altitude change to the horizontal distance between any two points on the line.

a. Slope0
b. Thing
c. Undefined
d. Undefined

78. _____ is a list of goods and materials, or those goods and materials themselves, held available in stock by a business
a. Thing
b. Inventory0
c. Undefined
d. Undefined

Chapter 8. Rational Expressions

1. An _____ is a combination of numbers, operators, grouping symbols and/or free variables and bound variables arranged in a meaningful way which can be evaluated..
   - a. Expression0
   - b. Thing
   - c. Undefined
   - d. Undefined

2. In mathematics, a _____ is the end result of a division problem. It can also be expressed as the number of times the divisor divides into the dividend.
   - a. Thing
   - b. Quotient0
   - c. Undefined
   - d. Undefined

3. In mathematics, a _____ number is a number which can be expressed as a ratio of two integers. Non-integer _____ numbers (commonly called fractions) are usually written as the vulgar fraction a / b, where b is not zero.
   - a. Thing
   - b. Rational0
   - c. Undefined
   - d. Undefined

4. In mathematics, a _____ is an expression that is constructed from one or more variables and constants, using only the operations of addition, subtraction, multiplication, and constant positive whole number exponents. is a _____. Note in particular that division by an expression containing a variable is not in general allowed in polynomials. [1]
   - a. Thing
   - b. Polynomial0
   - c. Undefined
   - d. Undefined

5. In geographic information systems, a _____ comprises an entity with a geographic location, typically determined by points, arcs, or polygons. Carriageways and cadastres exemplify _____ data.
   - a. Feature0
   - b. Thing
   - c. Undefined
   - d. Undefined

6. In mathematics, defined and _____ are used to explain whether or not expressions have meaningful, sensible, and unambiguous values.
   - a. Thing
   - b. Undefined0
   - c. Undefined
   - d. Undefined

7. A _____ is the part of a fraction that tells how many equal parts make up a whole, and which is used in the name of the fraction: "halves", "thirds", "fourths" or "quarters", "fifths" and so on.
   - a. Concept
   - b. Denominator0
   - c. Undefined
   - d. Undefined

8. A _____ is a symbolic representation denoting a quantity or expression. It often represents an "unknown" quantity that has the potential to change.
   - a. Variable0
   - b. Thing
   - c. Undefined
   - d. Undefined

9. _____ the expected value of a random variable displays the average or central value of the variable.It is a summary value of the distribution of the variable.
   - a. Thing
   - b. Determining0
   - c. Undefined
   - d. Undefined

Chapter 8. Rational Expressions

10. _____ are the basic objects of study in graph theory. Informally speaking, a graph is a set of objects called points, nodes, or vertices connected by links called lines or edges.
    a. Thing
    b. Graphs0
    c. Undefined
    d. Undefined

11. In geometry, a _____ is defined as a quadrilateral where all four of its angles are right angles.
    a. Thing
    b. Rectangle0
    c. Undefined
    d. Undefined

12. In statistics, _____ means the most frequent value assumed by a random variable, or occurring in a sampling of a random variable.
    a. Concept
    b. Mode0
    c. Undefined
    d. Undefined

13. In mathematics, _____ expressions is used to reduce the expression into the lowest possible term.
    a. Thing
    b. Simplifying0
    c. Undefined
    d. Undefined

14. A _____ is a numeral used to indicate a count. The most common use of the word today is to name the part of a fraction that tells the number or count of equal parts.
    a. Numerator0
    b. Thing
    c. Undefined
    d. Undefined

15. _____ is the largest positive integer that divides both numbers without remainder.
    a. Common Factor0
    b. Thing
    c. Undefined
    d. Undefined

16. In mathematics, factorization (British English: factorisation) or factoring is the decomposition of an object (for example, a number, a polynomial, or a matrix) into a product of other objects, or _____, which when multiplied together give the original.
    a. Thing
    b. Factors0
    c. Undefined
    d. Undefined

17. A _____ is a negotiable instrument instructing a financial institution to pay a specific amount of a specific currency from a specific demand account held in the maker/depositor's name with that institution. Both the maker and payee may be natural persons or legal entities.
    a. Check0
    b. Thing
    c. Undefined
    d. Undefined

18. In mathematics, a _____ may be described informally as a number that can be given by an infinite decimal representation.
    a. Real number0
    b. Thing
    c. Undefined
    d. Undefined

19. In linear algebra, the _____ of an n-by-n square matrix A is defined to be the sum of the elements on the main diagonal of A,

a. Trace0
c. Undefined
b. Thing
d. Undefined

20. The _____ is a property of multiplication or addition where the product or sum remains the same, regardless of whether or not the order of the addends or factors are changed.
   a. Thing
   b. Commutative property0
   c. Undefined
   d. Undefined

21. In mathematics, the additive inverse, or _____ of a number n is the number that, when added to n, yields zero. The additive inverse of n is denoted −n. For example, 7 is −7, because 7 + (−7) = 0, and the additive inverse of −0.3 is 0.3, because −0.3 + 0.3 = 0.
   a. Opposite0
   b. Thing
   c. Undefined
   d. Undefined

22. In mathematics, the _____ of a number n is the number that, when added to n, yields zero. The _____ of n is denoted −n. For example, 7 is −7, because 7 + (−7) = 0, and the _____ of −0.3 is 0.3, because −0.3 + 0.3 = 0.
   a. Thing
   b. Additive inverse0
   c. Undefined
   d. Undefined

23. _____ is a kind of property which exists as magnitude or multitude. It is among the basic classes of things along with quality, substance, change, and relation.
   a. Amount0
   b. Thing
   c. Undefined
   d. Undefined

24. _____ is a way of expressing a number as a fraction of 100 per cent meaning "per hundred".
   a. Thing
   b. Percent0
   c. Undefined
   d. Undefined

25. _____ is the application of tools and a processing medium to the transformation of raw materials into finished goods for sale.
   a. Thing
   b. Manufacturing0
   c. Undefined
   d. Undefined

26. A _____ is a special kind of ratio, indicating a relationship between two measurements with different units, such as miles to gallons or cents to pounds.
   a. Thing
   b. Rate0
   c. Undefined
   d. Undefined

27. _____ means in succession or back-to-back
   a. Thing
   b. Consecutive0
   c. Undefined
   d. Undefined

28. A _____ of a number is the product of that number with any integer.
   a. Multiple0
   b. Thing
   c. Undefined
   d. Undefined

29. In mathematics, a _____ is the result of multiplying, or an expression that identifies factors to be multiplied.
   a. Thing
   b. Product0
   c. Undefined
   d. Undefined

30. In mathematics, the _____ inverse of a number x, denoted 1/x or x^{-1}, is the number which, when multiplied by x, yields 1. The _____ inverse of x is also called the reciprocal of x.
   a. Multiplicative0
   b. Thing
   c. Undefined
   d. Undefined

31. _____ element of an element x with respect to a binary operation * with identity element e is an element y such that x * y = y * x = e. In particular,
   a. Inverse0
   b. Thing
   c. Undefined
   d. Undefined

32. In mathematics, _____ is an elementary arithmetic operation. When one of the numbers is a whole number, _____ is the repeated sum of the other number.
   a. Multiplication0
   b. Thing
   c. Undefined
   d. Undefined

33. In mathematics, a _____ of an integer n, also called a factor of n, is an integer which evenly divides n without leaving a remainder.
   a. Thing
   b. Divisor0
   c. Undefined
   d. Undefined

34. In mathematics, a _____ is a number which can be expressed as a ratio of two integers. Non-integer rational numbers (commonly called fractions) are usually written as the vulgar fraction a / b, where b is not zero.
   a. Rational Number0
   b. Concept
   c. Undefined
   d. Undefined

35. A _____ is the result of the addition of a set of numbers. The numbers may be natural numbers, complex numbers, matrices, or still more complicated objects. An infinite _____ is a subtle procedure known as a series.
   a. Sum0
   b. Thing
   c. Undefined
   d. Undefined

36. _____, either of the curved-bracket punctuation marks that together make a set of _____
   a. Parentheses0
   b. Thing
   c. Undefined
   d. Undefined

37. In mathematics, the _____ inverse, or opposite, of a number n is the number that, when added to n, yields zero. The _____ inverse of n is denoted −n.
   a. Thing
   b. Additive0
   c. Undefined
   d. Undefined

38. _____ has many meanings, most of which simply .

Chapter 8. Rational Expressions

a. Thing
b. Power0
c. Undefined
d. Undefined

39. _____ is a physical property of a system that underlies the common notions of hot and cold; something that is hotter has the greater _____.
   a. Temperature0
   b. Thing
   c. Undefined
   d. Undefined

40. _____ is the distance around a given two-dimensional object. As a general rule, the _____ of a polygon can always be calculated by adding all the length of the sides together. So, the formula for triangles is P = a + b + c, where a, b and c stand for each side of it. For quadrilaterals the equation is P = a + b + c + d. For equilateral polygons, P = na, where n is the number of sides and a is the side length.
   a. Thing
   b. Perimeter0
   c. Undefined
   d. Undefined

41. Statistical _____ is a statistical procedure in which individual items are placed into groups based on quantitative information on one or more characteristics inherent in the items and based on a training set of previously labeled items.
   a. Classification0
   b. Thing
   c. Undefined
   d. Undefined

42. _____ or arithmetics is the oldest and most elementary branch of mathematics, used by almost everyone, for tasks ranging from simple daily counting to advanced science and business calculations.
   a. Thing
   b. Arithmetic0
   c. Undefined
   d. Undefined

43. Equivalence is the condition of being _____ or essentially equal.
   a. Equivalent0
   b. Thing
   c. Undefined
   d. Undefined

44. In mathematics, a _____ number (or a _____) is a natural number that has exactly two (distinct) natural number divisors, which are 1 and the _____ number itself.
   a. Prime0
   b. Thing
   c. Undefined
   d. Undefined

45. In abstract algebra, _____ consists of sets with binary operations that satisfy certain axioms.
   a. Thing
   b. Grouping0
   c. Undefined
   d. Undefined

46. In mathematics, and in particular in abstract algebra, the _____ is a property of binary operations that generalises the distributive law from elementary algebra.
   a. Distributive property0
   b. Thing
   c. Undefined
   d. Undefined

47. In mathematics, _____ is the decomposition of an object into a product of other objects, or factors, which when multiplied together give the original.

Chapter 8. Rational Expressions

a. Factoring0
b. Thing
c. Undefined
d. Undefined

48. _____ also sometimes known as the double distributive property or more colloquially as foiling, is commonly taught to US high school students learning algebra as a mnemonic for remembering how to multiply two binomials polynomials with two terms.
a. Thing
b. FOIL method0
c. Undefined
d. Undefined

49. The _____ is commonly taught to US high school students learning algebra as a mnemonic for remembering how to multiply two binomials.
a. FOIL rule0
b. Thing
c. Undefined
d. Undefined

50. A _____ fraction is a fraction in which the absolute value of the numerator is less than the denominator--hence, the absolute value of the fraction is less than 1.
a. Thing
b. Proper0
c. Undefined
d. Undefined

51. The _____, the average in everyday English, which is also called the arithmetic _____ (and is distinguished from the geometric _____ or harmonic _____). The average is also called the sample _____. The expected value of a random variable, which is also called the population _____.
a. Thing
b. Mean0
c. Undefined
d. Undefined

52. _____ is often used to describe the measurement of the steepness, incline, gradient, or grade of a straight line. The _____ is defined as the ratio of the "rise" divided by the "run" between two points on a line, or in other words, the ratio of the altitude change to the horizontal distance between any two points on the line.
a. Thing
b. Slope0
c. Undefined
d. Undefined

53. In mathematics, an _____, mean, or central tendency of a data set refers to a measure of the "middle" or "expected" value of the data set.
a. Average0
b. Concept
c. Undefined
d. Undefined

54. The _____ (symbol _____) and the millibar (symbol mbar, also mb) are units of pressure.
a. Bar0
b. Thing
c. Undefined
d. Undefined

55. A _____ is a unit of length, usually used to measure distance, in a number of different systems, including Imperial units, United States customary units and Norwegian/Swedish mil. Its size can vary from system to system, but in each is between 1 and 10 kilometers. In contemporary English contexts _____ refers to either:
a. Thing
b. Mile0
c. Undefined
d. Undefined

Chapter 8. Rational Expressions

56. _____ is a unit of speed, expressing the number of international miles covered per hour.
   a. Thing
   b. Miles per hour0
   c. Undefined
   d. Undefined

57. In geometry, the _____ of an object is a point in some sense in the middle of the object.
   a. Center0
   b. Thing
   c. Undefined
   d. Undefined

58. In mathematics, the _____ of two sets A and B is the set that contains all elements of A that also belong to B (or equivalently, all elements of B that also belong to A), but no other elements.
   a. Intersection0
   b. Thing
   c. Undefined
   d. Undefined

59. In mathematics and the mathematical sciences, a _____ is a fixed, but possibly unspecified, value. This is in contrast to a variable, which is not fixed.
   a. Constant0
   b. Thing
   c. Undefined
   d. Undefined

60. _____ is a fixed, but possibly unspecified, value. This is in contrast to a variable, which is not fixed.
   a. Thing
   b. Constant term0
   c. Undefined
   d. Undefined

61. _____ is a list of goods and materials, or those goods and materials themselves, held available in stock by a business
   a. Inventory0
   b. Thing
   c. Undefined
   d. Undefined

62. A _____ is a set of numbers that designate location in a given reference system, such as x,y in a planar _____ system or an x,y,z in a three-dimensional _____ system.
   a. Coordinate0
   b. Thing
   c. Undefined
   d. Undefined

63. In sociology and biology a _____ is the collection of people or organisms of a particular species living in a given geographic area or space, usually measured by a census.
   a. Population0
   b. Thing
   c. Undefined
   d. Undefined

64. _____ is the transport of people on a trip/journey or the process or time involved in a person or object moving from one location to another.
   a. Travel0
   b. Thing
   c. Undefined
   d. Undefined

65. A _____ is one of the basic shapes of geometry: a polygon with three vertices and three sides which are straight line segments.

Chapter 8. Rational Expressions

   a. Thing
   c. Undefined
   b. Triangle0
   d. Undefined

66. In finance, a _____ is collateral that the holder of a position in securities, options, or futures contracts has to deposit to cover the credit risk of his counterparty.
   a. Thing
   c. Undefined
   b. Margin0
   d. Undefined

67. In Euclidean geometry, a uniform _____ is a linear transformation that enlargers or diminishes objects, and whose _____ factor is the same in all directions. This is also called homothethy.
   a. Thing
   c. Undefined
   b. Scale0
   d. Undefined

68. _____ (i.e. Plans) are a set of two-dimensional diagrams or _____ used to describe a place or object, or to communicate building or fabrication instructions.
   a. Drawings0
   c. Undefined
   b. Thing
   d. Undefined

69. A _____ is a function that assigns a number to subsets of a given set.
   a. Thing
   c. Undefined
   b. Measure0
   d. Undefined

70. In mathematics, there are several meanings of _____ depending on the subject.
   a. Degree0
   c. Undefined
   b. Thing
   d. Undefined

71. In mathematics, two quantities are called _____ if they vary in such a way that one of the quantities is a constant multiple of the other, or equivalently if they have a constant ratio.
   a. Proportional0
   c. Undefined
   b. Thing
   d. Undefined

72. The metre (or _____, see spelling differences) is a measure of length. It is the basic unit of length in the metric system and in the International System of Units (SI), used around the world for general and scientific purposes.
   a. Meter0
   c. Undefined
   b. Concept
   d. Undefined

73. In mathematics, an _____ on a real vector space is a choice of which ordered bases are "positively" oriented, or right-handed, and which are "negatively" oriented, or left-handed.
   a. Orientation0
   c. Undefined
   b. Thing
   d. Undefined

74. _____ forms part of thinking. Considered the most complex of all intellectual functions, _____ has been defined as higher-order cognitive process that requires the modulation and control of more routine or fundamental skills.
   a. Thing
   c. Undefined
   b. Problem solving0
   d. Undefined

75. _____ is electromagnetic radiation with a wavelength that is visible to the eye (visible _____) or, in a technical or scientific context, electromagnetic radiation of any wavelength.
   a. Light0
   b. Thing
   c. Undefined
   d. Undefined

76. In mathematics and logic, a _____ proof is a way of showing the truth or falsehood of a given statement by a straightforward combination of established facts, usually existing lemmas and theorems, without making any further assumptions.
   a. Thing
   b. Direct0
   c. Undefined
   d. Undefined

77. _____ is the relationship between two variables, like a ratio in which the two quantities being compared are different units.
   a. Direct variation0
   b. Thing
   c. Undefined
   d. Undefined

78. _____ is a form of periodic payment from an employer to an employee, which is specified in an employment contract.
   a. Thing
   b. Gross pay0
   c. Undefined
   d. Undefined

79. A _____ is a form of periodic payment from an employer to an employee, which is specified in an employment contract.
   a. Salary0
   b. Thing
   c. Undefined
   d. Undefined

80. In common philosophical language, a proposition or _____, is the content of an assertion, that is, it is true-or-false and defined by the meaning of a particular piece of language.
   a. Concept
   b. Statement0
   c. Undefined
   d. Undefined

81. _____ is a state in the southern region of the United States of America and was one of the original Thirteen Colonies that revolted against British rule in the American Revolution.
   a. Thing
   b. Georgia0
   c. Undefined
   d. Undefined

82. The _____ of a solid object is the three-dimensional concept of how much space it occupies, often quantified numerically.
   a. Volume0
   b. Thing
   c. Undefined
   d. Undefined

83. In plane geometry, a _____ is a polygon with four equal sides, four right angles, and parallel opposite sides. In algebra, the _____ of a number is that number multiplied by itself.
   a. Square0
   b. Thing
   c. Undefined
   d. Undefined

Chapter 8. Rational Expressions

84. _____ is a subset of a population.
   a. Thing
   b. Sample0
   c. Undefined
   d. Undefined

85. _____ are a measure of time.
   a. Thing
   b. Minutes0
   c. Undefined
   d. Undefined

86. The _____ or kilogramme is the SI base unit of mass. It is defined as being equal to the mass of the international prototype of the _____.
   a. Thing
   b. Kilogram0
   c. Undefined
   d. Undefined

87. A _____ is a dimensionless measure of relative speed.
   a. Thing
   b. Mach number0
   c. Undefined
   d. Undefined

88. _____ is the estimation of a physical quantity such as distance, energy, temperature, or time.
   a. Thing
   b. Measurement0
   c. Undefined
   d. Undefined

89. The _____, in practice often shortened to amp, is a unit of electric current, or amount of electric charge per second.
   a. Amperes0
   b. Thing
   c. Undefined
   d. Undefined

90. In mathematics, the _____ of a function is the set of all "output" values produced by that function. Given a function $f : A \to B$, the _____ of f, is defined to be the set {x $\in$ B:x=f(a) for some a $\in$ A}.
   a. Thing
   b. Range0
   c. Undefined
   d. Undefined

91. The word _____ is used in a variety of ways in mathematics.
   a. Thing
   b. Index0
   c. Undefined
   d. Undefined

92. In mathematics, a _____ can mean either an element of the set {1, 2, 3, ...} (i.e the positive integers) or an element of the set {0, 1, 2, 3, ...} (i.e. the non-negative integers).
   a. Concept
   b. Whole number0
   c. Undefined
   d. Undefined

93. _____ is the fee paid on borrowed money.
   a. Interest0
   b. Thing
   c. Undefined
   d. Undefined

94. In economics, supply and _____ describe market relations between prospective sellers and buyers of a good.

96 Chapter 8. Rational Expressions

a. Thing
b. Demand0
c. Undefined
d. Undefined

95. In the scientific method, an _____ (Latin: ex-+-periri, "of (or from) trying"), is a set of actions and observations, performed in the context of solving a particular problem or question, in order to support or falsify a hypothesis or research concerning phenomena.
a. Thing
b. Experiment0
c. Undefined
d. Undefined

96. _____ refers to all non-domesticated plants, animals, and other organisms.
a. Wildlife0
b. Thing
c. Undefined
d. Undefined

97. _____ is a term used in marketing to indicate how much the price of a product is above the cost of producing and distributing the product.
a. Thing
b. Markup0
c. Undefined
d. Undefined

98. In mathematics and its applications, a _____ is a system for assigning an n-tuple of numbers or scalars to each point in an n-dimensional space.
a. Coordinate system0
b. Concept
c. Undefined
d. Undefined

99. In mathematics, an _____ is a statement about the relative size or order of two objects.
a. Inequality0
b. Thing
c. Undefined
d. Undefined

100. A _____ is the part of the dividend that is left over when the dividend is not evenly divisible by the divisor.
a. Thing
b. Remainder0
c. Undefined
d. Undefined

101. _____ is a synonym for information.
a. Thing
b. Data0
c. Undefined
d. Undefined

102. _____ is the symbold used to indicate the nth root of a number
a. Thing
b. Radical0
c. Undefined
d. Undefined

103. In mathematics, _____ are used to indicate the square root of a number.
a. Radicals0
b. Thing
c. Undefined
d. Undefined

104. In mathematics, a _____ of a complex-valued function f is a member x of the domain of f such that f(x) vanishes at x, that is, $x : f(x) = 0$.

a. Root0
b. Thing
c. Undefined
d. Undefined

105. In mathematics, _____ is a part of the set theoretic notion of function.
a. Thing
b. Image0
c. Undefined
d. Undefined

Chapter 9. Roots and Radicals

1. In classical geometry, a _____ of a circle or sphere is any line segment from its center to its boundary. By extension, the _____ of a circle or sphere is the length of any such segment. The _____ is half the diameter. In science and engineering the term _____ of curvature is commonly used as a synonym for _____.
   - a. Thing
   - b. Radius0
   - c. Undefined
   - d. Undefined

2. An _____ is a combination of numbers, operators, grouping symbols and/or free variables and bound variables arranged in a meaningful way which can be evaluated..
   - a. Thing
   - b. Expression0
   - c. Undefined
   - d. Undefined

3. A _____ is a unit of length, usually used to measure distance, in a number of different systems, including Imperial units, United States customary units and Norwegian/Swedish mil. Its size can vary from system to system, but in each is between 1 and 10 kilometers. In contemporary English contexts _____ refers to either:
   - a. Mile0
   - b. Thing
   - c. Undefined
   - d. Undefined

4. _____ is a unit of speed, expressing the number of international miles covered per hour.
   - a. Thing
   - b. Miles per hour0
   - c. Undefined
   - d. Undefined

5. The _____ in a vacuum is an important physical constant denoted by the letter c for constant or the Latin word celeritas meaning "swiftness
   - a. Speed of light0
   - b. Thing
   - c. Undefined
   - d. Undefined

6. _____ is electromagnetic radiation with a wavelength that is visible to the eye (visible _____) or, in a technical or scientific context, electromagnetic radiation of any wavelength.
   - a. Thing
   - b. Light0
   - c. Undefined
   - d. Undefined

7. In mathematics, a _____ of a complex-valued function f is a member x of the domain of f such that f(x) vanishes at x, that is, x : f (x) = 0.
   - a. Thing
   - b. Root0
   - c. Undefined
   - d. Undefined

8. _____ (March 14, 1879 - April 18, 1955) was a German-born theoretical physicist who is best known for his theory of relativity and specifically mass-energy equivalence, $E = mc^2$.
   - a. Person
   - b. Albert Einstein0
   - c. Undefined
   - d. Undefined

9. _____ is the symbold used to indicate the nth root of a number
   - a. Thing
   - b. Radical0
   - c. Undefined
   - d. Undefined

10. In mathematics, _____ are used to indicate the square root of a number.

Chapter 9. Roots and Radicals

    a. Thing
    b. Radicals0
    c. Undefined
    d. Undefined

11. In plane geometry, a _____ is a polygon with four equal sides, four right angles, and parallel opposite sides. In algebra, the _____ of a number is that number multiplied by itself.
    a. Thing
    b. Square0
    c. Undefined
    d. Undefined

12. In mathematics, a _____ of a number x is a number r such that $r^2 = x$, or in words, a number r whose square (the result of multiplying the number by itself) is x.
    a. Square root0
    b. Thing
    c. Undefined
    d. Undefined

13. _____ is a mathematical operation, written a^n, involving two numbers, the base a and the exponent n.
    a. Exponentiating0
    b. Thing
    c. Undefined
    d. Undefined

14. _____ is a mathematical operation, written a^n, involving two numbers, the base a and the exponent n.
    a. Thing
    b. Exponentiation0
    c. Undefined
    d. Undefined

15. The _____ integers are all the integers from zero on upwards.
    a. Thing
    b. Nonnegative0
    c. Undefined
    d. Undefined

16. The _____ is the number or expression underneath the radical sign.
    a. Thing
    b. Radicand0
    c. Undefined
    d. Undefined

17. In mathematics, an _____ number is any real number that is not a rational number- that is, it is a number which cannot be expressed as a fraction m/n, where m and n are integers.
    a. Irrational0
    b. Thing
    c. Undefined
    d. Undefined

18. In mathematics, a _____ may be described informally as a number that can be given by an infinite decimal representation.
    a. Real number0
    b. Thing
    c. Undefined
    d. Undefined

19. A _____ is a negotiable instrument instructing a financial institution to pay a specific amount of a specific currency from a specific demand account held in the maker/depositor's name with that institution. Both the maker and payee may be natural persons or legal entities.
    a. Check0
    b. Thing
    c. Undefined
    d. Undefined

20. A _____ is an abstract model that uses mathematical language to describe the behavior of a system. Eykhoff defined a _____ as 'a representation of the essential aspects of an existing system which presents knowledge of that system in usable form'.
   a. Mathematical model0
   b. Thing
   c. Undefined
   d. Undefined

21. _____ is a term applied when talking about the movement of air from one place to the next.
   a. Thing
   b. Wind speed0
   c. Undefined
   d. Undefined

22. In mathematics, an _____, mean, or central tendency of a data set refers to a measure of the "middle" or "expected" value of the data set.
   a. Concept
   b. Average0
   c. Undefined
   d. Undefined

23. _____ is a kind of property which exists as magnitude or multitude. It is among the basic classes of things along with quality, substance, change, and relation.
   a. Amount0
   b. Thing
   c. Undefined
   d. Undefined

24. _____ is a synonym for information.
   a. Data0
   b. Thing
   c. Undefined
   d. Undefined

25. In mathematics, a _____ number is a number which can be expressed as a ratio of two integers. Non-integer _____ numbers (commonly called fractions) are usually written as the vulgar fraction a / b, where b is not zero.
   a. Thing
   b. Rational0
   c. Undefined
   d. Undefined

26. The term _____ can refer to an integer which is the square of some other integer, or an algebraic expression that can be factored as the square of some other expression.
   a. Perfect square0
   b. Thing
   c. Undefined
   d. Undefined

27. In mathematics, a _____ is the end result of a division problem. It can also be expressed as the number of times the divisor divides into the dividend.
   a. Quotient0
   b. Thing
   c. Undefined
   d. Undefined

28. The _____ are the only integral domain whose positive elements are well-ordered, and in which order is preserved by addition. Like the natural numbers, the _____ form a countably infinite set. The set of all _____ is usually denoted in mathematics by a boldface Z .
   a. Integers0
   b. Thing
   c. Undefined
   d. Undefined

Chapter 9. Roots and Radicals

29. In mathematics, an _____ is any real number that is not a rational number ¡ª that is, it is a number which cannot be expressed as m/n, where m and n are integers.
    a. Thing
    b. Irrational number0
    c. Undefined
    d. Undefined

30. A _____ is a number that is less than zero.
    a. Negative number0
    b. Thing
    c. Undefined
    d. Undefined

31. In mathematics, an inequality is a statement about the relative size or order of two objects. For example 14 > 10, or 14 is _____ 10.
    a. Greater than0
    b. Thing
    c. Undefined
    d. Undefined

32. The word _____ is used in a variety of ways in mathematics.
    a. Thing
    b. Index0
    c. Undefined
    d. Undefined

33. A _____ is a three-dimensional solid object bounded by six square faces, facets, or sides, with three meeting at each vertex.
    a. Thing
    b. Cube0
    c. Undefined
    d. Undefined

34. A _____ of a number is a number a such that $a^3 = x$.
    a. Thing
    b. Cube root0
    c. Undefined
    d. Undefined

35. A _____ is 360° or 2ð radians.
    a. Turn0
    b. Thing
    c. Undefined
    d. Undefined

36. _____ of an object is its speed in a particular direction.
    a. Thing
    b. Velocity0
    c. Undefined
    d. Undefined

37. _____ is the transport of people on a trip/journey or the process or time involved in a person or object moving from one location to another.
    a. Travel0
    b. Thing
    c. Undefined
    d. Undefined

38. In mathematics, _____ refers to a number of loosely related concepts in different areas of geometry. Intuitively, _____ is the amount by which a geometric object deviates from being flat, but this is defined in different ways depending on the context
    a. Thing
    b. Curvature0
    c. Undefined
    d. Undefined

39. In mathematics, the concept of a _____ tries to capture the intuitive idea of a geometrical one-dimensional and continuous object. A simple example is the circle.
    a. Curve0
    b. Thing
    c. Undefined
    d. Undefined

40. A _____ is a function that assigns a number to subsets of a given set.
    a. Measure0
    b. Thing
    c. Undefined
    d. Undefined

41. In probability theory and statistics, a _____ is a number dividing the higher half of a sample, a population, or a probability distribution from the lower half.
    a. Concept
    b. Median0
    c. Undefined
    d. Undefined

42. In geometry, a _____ is defined as a quadrilateral where all four of its angles are right angles.
    a. Rectangle0
    b. Thing
    c. Undefined
    d. Undefined

43. A _____ is a one-dimensional picture in which the integers are shown as specially-marked points evenly spaced on a line.
    a. Number line0
    b. Thing
    c. Undefined
    d. Undefined

44. In mathematics, a _____ is the result of multiplying, or an expression that identifies factors to be multiplied.
    a. Product0
    b. Thing
    c. Undefined
    d. Undefined

45. The _____ is a method of finding the derivative of a function that is the quotient of two other functions for which derivatives exist.
    a. Quotient rule0
    b. Thing
    c. Undefined
    d. Undefined

46. The _____ governs the differentiation of products of differentiable functions.
    a. Product rule0
    b. Thing
    c. Undefined
    d. Undefined

47. In mathematics, a _____ is a number which can be expressed as a ratio of two integers. Non-integer rational numbers (commonly called fractions) are usually written as the vulgar fraction a / b, where b is not zero.
    a. Rational Number0
    b. Concept
    c. Undefined
    d. Undefined

48. In mathematics, _____ expressions is used to reduce the expression into the lowest possible term.
    a. Simplifying0
    b. Thing
    c. Undefined
    d. Undefined

Chapter 9. Roots and Radicals

49. In mathematics, factorization (British English: factorisation) or factoring is the decomposition of an object (for example, a number, a polynomial, or a matrix) into a product of other objects, or _____, which when multiplied together give the original.
    a. Factors0
    b. Thing
    c. Undefined
    d. Undefined

50. The _____, the average in everyday English, which is also called the arithmetic _____ (and is distinguished from the geometric _____ or harmonic _____). The average is also called the sample _____. The expected value of a random variable, which is also called the population _____.
    a. Mean0
    b. Thing
    c. Undefined
    d. Undefined

51. A _____ is a symbolic representation denoting a quantity or expression. It often represents an "unknown" quantity that has the potential to change.
    a. Variable0
    b. Thing
    c. Undefined
    d. Undefined

52. _____ has many meanings, most of which simply .
    a. Power0
    b. Thing
    c. Undefined
    d. Undefined

53. A _____ is a special kind of ratio, indicating a relationship between two measurements with different units, such as miles to gallons or cents to pounds.
    a. Rate0
    b. Thing
    c. Undefined
    d. Undefined

54. _____ is a set, with some particular properties and usually some additional structure, such as the operations of addition or multiplication, for instance.
    a. Space0
    b. Thing
    c. Undefined
    d. Undefined

55. An _____ of a number a is a number b such that $b^n=a$.
    a. Nth root0
    b. Thing
    c. Undefined
    d. Undefined

56. The _____ is defined as the summation of all particles and energy that exist and the space-time which all events occur.
    a. Universe0
    b. Thing
    c. Undefined
    d. Undefined

57. In mathematics, a _____ is an expression that is constructed from one or more variables and constants, using only the operations of addition, subtraction, multiplication, and constant positive whole number exponents. is a _____. Note in particular that division by an expression containing a variable is not in general allowed in polynomials. [1]
    a. Polynomial0
    b. Thing
    c. Undefined
    d. Undefined

Chapter 9. Roots and Radicals

58. In mathematics, _____ is an elementary arithmetic operation. When one of the numbers is a whole number, _____ is the repeated sum of the other number.
    a. Thing
    b. Multiplication0
    c. Undefined
    d. Undefined

59. _____ also sometimes known as the double distributive property or more colloquially as foiling, is commonly taught to US high school students learning algebra as a mnemonic for remembering how to multiply two binomials polynomials with two terms.
    a. FOIL method0
    b. Thing
    c. Undefined
    d. Undefined

60. The _____ is commonly taught to US high school students learning algebra as a mnemonic for remembering how to multiply two binomials.
    a. FOIL rule0
    b. Thing
    c. Undefined
    d. Undefined

61. In mathematics, and in particular in abstract algebra, the _____ is a property of binary operations that generalises the distributive law from elementary algebra.
    a. Thing
    b. Distributive property0
    c. Undefined
    d. Undefined

62. A _____ is the result of the addition of a set of numbers. The numbers may be natural numbers, complex numbers, matrices, or still more complicated objects. An infinite _____ is a subtle procedure known as a series.
    a. Sum0
    b. Thing
    c. Undefined
    d. Undefined

63. In algebra, a _____ is a binomial formed by taking the opposite of the second term of a binomial.
    a. Thing
    b. Conjugate0
    c. Undefined
    d. Undefined

64. _____ is a physical property of a system that underlies the common notions of hot and cold; something that is hotter has the greater _____.
    a. Temperature0
    b. Thing
    c. Undefined
    d. Undefined

65. _____ is a temperature scale named after the German physicist Daniel Gabriel _____ , who proposed it in 1724.
    a. Thing
    b. Fahrenheit0
    c. Undefined
    d. Undefined

66. In mathematics, there are several meanings of _____ depending on the subject.
    a. Degree0
    b. Thing
    c. Undefined
    d. Undefined

Chapter 9. Roots and Radicals

67. _____ is the distance around a given two-dimensional object. As a general rule, the _____ of a polygon can always be calculated by adding all the length of the sides together. So, the formula for triangles is P = a + b + c, where a, b and c stand for each side of it. For quadrilaterals the equation is P = a + b + c + d. For equilateral polygons, P = na, where n is the number of sides and a is the side length.
- a. Thing
- b. Perimeter0
- c. Undefined
- d. Undefined

68. In common philosophical language, a proposition or _____, is the content of an assertion, that is, it is true-or-false and defined by the meaning of a particular piece of language.
- a. Statement0
- b. Concept
- c. Undefined
- d. Undefined

69. _____, or Rationalisation in mathematics is the process of removing a square root or imaginary number from the denominator of a fraction.
- a. Thing
- b. Rationalizing0
- c. Undefined
- d. Undefined

70. A _____ is the part of a fraction that tells how many equal parts make up a whole, and which is used in the name of the fraction: "halves", "thirds", "fourths" or "quarters", "fifths" and so on.
- a. Concept
- b. Denominator0
- c. Undefined
- d. Undefined

71. In mathematics, a _____ can mean either an element of the set {1, 2, 3, ...} (i.e the positive integers or the counting numbers) or an element of the set {0, 1, 2, 3, ...} (i.e. the non-negative integers).
- a. Thing
- b. Natural number0
- c. Undefined
- d. Undefined

72. A _____ is a numeral used to indicate a count. The most common use of the word today is to name the part of a fraction that tells the number or count of equal parts.
- a. Numerator0
- b. Thing
- c. Undefined
- d. Undefined

73. _____ is the largest positive integer that divides both numbers without remainder.
- a. Common Factor0
- b. Thing
- c. Undefined
- d. Undefined

74. In sociology and biology a _____ is the collection of people or organisms of a particular species living in a given geographic area or space, usually measured by a census.
- a. Population0
- b. Thing
- c. Undefined
- d. Undefined

75. In geographic information systems, a _____ comprises an entity with a geographic location, typically determined by points, arcs, or polygons. Carriageways and cadastres exemplify _____ data.
- a. Feature0
- b. Thing
- c. Undefined
- d. Undefined

Chapter 9. Roots and Radicals

76. A _____ is a rectangle whose side lengths are in the golden ratio, 1:, that is, approximately 1:1.618.
   a. Golden rectangle0
   b. Thing
   c. Undefined
   d. Undefined

77. A _____ is a quantity that denotes the proportional amount or magnitude of one quantity relative to another.
   a. Ratio0
   b. Thing
   c. Undefined
   d. Undefined

78. The word _____ comes from the Latin word linearis, which means created by lines.
   a. Thing
   b. Linear0
   c. Undefined
   d. Undefined

79. A _____ is an equation in which each term is either a constant or the product of a constant times the first power of a variable.
   a. Linear equation0
   b. Thing
   c. Undefined
   d. Undefined

80. In mathematics, _____ are the intuitive idea of a geometrical one-dimensional and continuous object.
   a. Curves0
   b. Thing
   c. Undefined
   d. Undefined

81. In mathematics, the _____ of two sets A and B is the set that contains all elements of A that also belong to B (or equivalently, all elements of B that also belong to A), but no other elements.
   a. Intersection0
   b. Thing
   c. Undefined
   d. Undefined

82. In mathematics, a _____ is a polynomial equation of the second degree. The general form is $ax^2 + bx + c = 0$.
   a. Quadratic equation0
   b. Thing
   c. Undefined
   d. Undefined

83. _____ variables are variables other than the independent variable that may bear any effect on the behavior of the subject being studied.
   a. Extraneous0
   b. Thing
   c. Undefined
   d. Undefined

84. A _____ is a unit of length in the metric system, equal to one thousand metres, the current SI base unit of length
   a. Thing
   b. Kilometer0
   c. Undefined
   d. Undefined

85. In geometry, an _____ of a triangle is a straight line through a vertex and perpendicular to (i.e. forming a right angle with) the opposite side or an extension of the opposite side.
   a. Altitude0
   b. Concept
   c. Undefined
   d. Undefined

86. The metre (or _____, see spelling differences) is a measure of length. It is the basic unit of length in the metric system and in the International System of Units (SI), used around the world for general and scientific purposes.

Chapter 9. Roots and Radicals

a. Concept
b. Meter0
c. Undefined
d. Undefined

87. In mathematics, a _____ is a two-dimensional manifold or surface that is perfectly flat.
   a. Plane0
   b. Thing
   c. Undefined
   d. Undefined

88. A _____ is an object that is attached to a pivot point so that it can swing freely.
   a. Thing
   b. Pendulum0
   c. Undefined
   d. Undefined

89. In geometry and trigonometry, a _____ is defined as an angle between two straight intersecting lines of ninety degrees, or one-quarter of a circle.
   a. Thing
   b. Right angle0
   c. Undefined
   d. Undefined

90. In physics, _____ is an influence that may cause an object to accelerate. It may be experienced as a lift, a push, or a pull. The actual acceleration of the body is determined by the vector sum of all forces acting on it, known as net _____ or resultant _____.
   a. Thing
   b. Force0
   c. Undefined
   d. Undefined

91. _____ means in succession or back-to-back
   a. Thing
   b. Consecutive0
   c. Undefined
   d. Undefined

92. A _____ is the part of the dividend that is left over when the dividend is not evenly divisible by the divisor.
   a. Thing
   b. Remainder0
   c. Undefined
   d. Undefined

93. _____ is the fee paid on borrowed money.
   a. Thing
   b. Interest0
   c. Undefined
   d. Undefined

94. _____, either of the curved-bracket punctuation marks that together make a set of _____
   a. Thing
   b. Parentheses0
   c. Undefined
   d. Undefined

95. _____, in economics and political economy, are the distributions or payments awarded to the various suppliers of the factors of production.
   a. Returns0
   b. Thing
   c. Undefined
   d. Undefined

96. The _____ (symbol _____) and the millibar (symbol mbar, also mb) are units of pressure.

a. Bar0
b. Thing
c. Undefined
d. Undefined

97. A bar chart, also known as a _____, is a chart with rectangular bars of lengths usually proportional to the magnitudes or frequencies of what they represent.
   a. Bar graph0
   b. Thing
   c. Undefined
   d. Undefined

98. In physics, a _____ may refer to the scalar _____ or to the vector _____.
   a. Potential0
   b. Thing
   c. Undefined
   d. Undefined

99. _____ is a way of expressing a number as a fraction of 100 per cent meaning "per hundred".
   a. Percent0
   b. Thing
   c. Undefined
   d. Undefined

100. Acid _____ ratio measures the ability of a company to use its near cash or quick assets to immediately extinguish its current liabilities.
   a. Thing
   b. Test0
   c. Undefined
   d. Undefined

101. The _____ of a solid object is the three-dimensional concept of how much space it occupies, often quantified numerically.
   a. Thing
   b. Volume0
   c. Undefined
   d. Undefined

102. The _____ of measurement are a globally standardized and modernized form of the metric system.
   a. Units0
   b. Thing
   c. Undefined
   d. Undefined

103. _____ are cubes in which all sides are of the same length and all face perpendicular to each other including an atom at each corner of the unigt cell.
   a. Cubic units0
   b. Thing
   c. Undefined
   d. Undefined

104. In mathematics, _____ are any real number that is not a rational number ¡ª that is, it is a number which cannot be expressed as m/n, where m and n are integers.
   a. Irrational numbers0
   b. Thing
   c. Undefined
   d. Undefined

105. _____ is the art and science of designing buildings and structures.
   a. Thing
   b. Architecture0
   c. Undefined
   d. Undefined

106. _____ (or proportionality) are two quantities that vary in such a way that one of the quatities is a constant multiple of the other, or equivalently if they have a constant ratio.

Chapter 9. Roots and Radicals

    a. Proportions0
    b. Thing
    c. Undefined
    d. Undefined

107. The _____ is a number often encountered when taking the ratios of distances in simple geometric figures. It is approximately 1.6180339887.
    a. Golden ratio0
    b. Thing
    c. Undefined
    d. Undefined

108. In business, particularly accounting, a _____ is the time intervals that the accounts, statement, payments, or other calculations cover.
    a. Thing
    b. Period0
    c. Undefined
    d. Undefined

109. A _____ is a landform that extends above the surrounding terrain in a limited area. A _____ is generally steeper than a hill, but there is no universally accepted standard definition for the height of a _____ or a hill although a _____ usually has an identifiable summit.
    a. Thing
    b. Mountain0
    c. Undefined
    d. Undefined

110. A _____ is a set of numbers that designate location in a given reference system, such as x,y in a planar _____ system or an x,y,z in a three-dimensional _____ system.
    a. Coordinate0
    b. Thing
    c. Undefined
    d. Undefined

111. In mathematics and its applications, a _____ is a system for assigning an n-tuple of numbers or scalars to each point in an n-dimensional space.
    a. Concept
    b. Coordinate system0
    c. Undefined
    d. Undefined

112. In mathematics, an _____ is a statement about the relative size or order of two objects.
    a. Thing
    b. Inequality0
    c. Undefined
    d. Undefined

113. _____ is often used to describe the measurement of the steepness, incline, gradient, or grade of a straight line. The _____ is defined as the ratio of the "rise" divided by the "run" between two points on a line, or in other words, the ratio of the altitude change to the horizontal distance between any two points on the line.
    a. Thing
    b. Slope0
    c. Undefined
    d. Undefined

114. _____ is a subset of a population.
    a. Sample0
    b. Thing
    c. Undefined
    d. Undefined

Chapter 10. Quadratic Equations and Functions

1. The most important measure of central tendency, and one of the basic building blocks of all statistical analysis, is the arithmetic _____. It is simply the sum of all the set of values divided by the number of values involved. As a measure of central tendency, it is affected by extreme scores, and it assumes a ratio scale of measurement.
   a. -equivalence
   b. Mean10
   c. Undefined
   d. Undefined

2. _____ is used synonymously for variable.
   a. -equivalence
   b. Factor10
   c. Undefined
   d. Undefined

3. A _____ is simply a polynomial with two terms.
   a. -equivalence
   b. Binomial10
   c. Undefined
   d. Undefined

4. A number that does not change in value in a given situation is a _____.
   a. -equivalence
   b. Constant10
   c. Undefined
   d. Undefined

5. The very fact that we are measuring objects with respect to some characteristic implies that the objects differ in that characteristic; or stated in another way, that the characteristic can take on a number of different values. These properties or characteristics of an object that can assume two or more different values are referred to as a _____.
   a. -equivalence
   b. Variable10
   c. Undefined
   d. Undefined

6. _____ are characteristics or properties of an object that can take on one or more different values.
   a. Variables10
   b. -equivalence
   c. Undefined
   d. Undefined

7. By _____ we mean collecting observations made upon our environment -- observations, which are the results of measurements using clocks, balances, measuring rods, counting operations, or other objectively defined measuring instruments or procedures. _____ may mean simply counting the number of times a particular property occurs.
   a. Data10
   b. -equivalence
   c. Undefined
   d. Undefined

8. _____ is implied when data values are distributed in the same way above and below the middle of the sample.
   a. -equivalence
   b. Symmetry10
   c. Undefined
   d. Undefined

9. The value of Y when X is 0 is the _____.
   a. ADE classification
   b. Intercept10
   c. Undefined
   d. Undefined

10. A measure of central tendency, the _____, corresponds to the point having 50% of the observations below it when observations are arranged in numerical order. The _____ assumes at least an interval level of measurement. For a symmetric distribution such as the normal distribution, the _____ is the same as the mean. For a distribution which is skewed to the right, the _____ is typically smaller than the mean or when skewed to the left, the _____ is smaller.

Chapter 10. Quadratic Equations and Functions

a. Median10
c. Undefined
b. -equivalence
d. Undefined

11. An _____ is any process or study, which results in the collection of data, the outcome of which is unknown. In statistics, the term is usually restricted to situations in which the researcher has control over some of the conditions under which the _____ takes place.
   a. ADE classification
   b. Experiment10
   c. Undefined
   d. Undefined

12. A measure of variability, the _____ is the distance from the lowest to the highest score.
   a. -equivalence
   b. Range10
   c. Undefined
   d. Undefined

13. An _____ is an indication of the value of an unknown quantity based on observed data. More formally, an _____ is the particular value of an estimator that is obtained from a particular sample of data and used to indicate the value of a parameter.
   a. ADE classification
   b. Estimate10
   c. Undefined
   d. Undefined

14. _____ refers to a useful summary of a set of bivariate data (two variables), usually drawn before working out a linear correlation coefficient or fitting a regression line. It gives a good visual picture of the relationship between the two variables, and aids the interpretation of the correlation coefficient or regression model.
   a. Scatter Plot10
   b. -equivalence
   c. Undefined
   d. Undefined

15. The _____ refers to the amount of change in Y for a 1 unit change in X; or in-other-words, the rate of change in the predicted value as a function of a change in the predictor variable.
   a. -equivalence
   b. Slope10
   c. Undefined
   d. Undefined

16. A graph in which the frequency of occurrence of different values of X is represented by the height of a bar is called a _____ .
   a. -equivalence
   b. Bar graph10
   c. Undefined
   d. Undefined

17. A _____ presents the Y values corresponding to different values of X and connects these values with a line.
   a. -equivalence
   b. Line graph10
   c. Undefined
   d. Undefined

18. _____ describes the phenomenon where the values of distribution tend to move towards the summary statistic. For example, values in a distribution tend to cluster about the mean, and in a linear _____ equation, they tend to cluster about the linear _____ equation.
   a. Regression10
   b. -equivalence
   c. Undefined
   d. Undefined

Chapter 1

1. b	2. b	3. b	4. a	5. a	6. b	7. b	8. a	9. b	10. a
11. b	12. b	13. b	14. a	15. b	16. a	17. b	18. b	19. b	20. b
21. b	22. a	23. b	24. a	25. a	26. a	27. b	28. a	29. b	30. b
31. a	32. a	33. b	34. b	35. a	36. b	37. a	38. a	39. b	40. b
41. a	42. a	43. a	44. b	45. b	46. b	47. a	48. b	49. a	50. a
51. a	52. b	53. b	54. a	55. a	56. a	57. a	58. a	59. b	60. a
61. b	62. b	63. b	64. b	65. b	66. b	67. b	68. b	69. b	70. a
71. a	72. b	73. b	74. b	75. a	76. a	77. a	78. a	79. a	80. a
81. b	82. a	83. b	84. b	85. a	86. b	87. a	88. a	89. b	90. b
91. b	92. b	93. b	94. a	95. b	96. b	97. a	98. a	99. b	100. b
101. b	102. b	103. a	104. b	105. a	106. b	107. a	108. a	109. a	110. b
111. b	112. a	113. a	114. a	115. a	116. b	117. a	118. a	119. b	120. a
121. a	122. b	123. b	124. b	125. b	126. a	127. b	128. a	129. a	130. b
131. b	132. a	133. a	134. b	135. b	136. a	137. b	138. a	139. b	140. b
141. b	142. a	143. b	144. b	145. a	146. b	147. b	148. a	149. a	150. a
151. a	152. a	153. a	154. a	155. b	156. a	157. b	158. a	159. a	160. a
161. a	162. b	163. a	164. b	165. b					

Chapter 2

1. b	2. b	3. b	4. b	5. a	6. b	7. a	8. b	9. a	10. a
11. a	12. a	13. b	14. a	15. a	16. a	17. a	18. a	19. a	20. b
21. b	22. b	23. a	24. b	25. a	26. b	27. b	28. a	29. a	30. b
31. a	32. b	33. a	34. a	35. a	36. b	37. b	38. b	39. a	40. a
41. b	42. b	43. b	44. a	45. a	46. a	47. b	48. a	49. b	50. a
51. a	52. b	53. a	54. b	55. b	56. a	57. a	58. a	59. a	60. b
61. a	62. a	63. b	64. a	65. b	66. a	67. b	68. a	69. b	70. b
71. a	72. a	73. b	74. b	75. b	76. a	77. a	78. a	79. a	80. a
81. b	82. b	83. a	84. b	85. a	86. a	87. a	88. a	89. a	90. a
91. b	92. b	93. b	94. a	95. b	96. b	97. a	98. b	99. a	100. a
101. b	102. b	103. a	104. a	105. b	106. a	107. a			

Chapter 3

1. a	2. b	3. a	4. b	5. b	6. b	7. a	8. b	9. b	10. b
11. a	12. b	13. b	14. b	15. a	16. a	17. a	18. b	19. b	20. b
21. a	22. a	23. a	24. b	25. a	26. a	27. b	28. a	29. a	30. b
31. b	32. a	33. b	34. a	35. b	36. b	37. a	38. b	39. a	40. a
41. a	42. b	43. a	44. b	45. b	46. b	47. a	48. a	49. a	50. a
51. a	52. b	53. b	54. a	55. a	56. a	57. b	58. a	59. a	60. b
61. b	62. b	63. b	64. b	65. a	66. b	67. b	68. a	69. a	70. a
71. b	72. a	73. b	74. b	75. b	76. b	77. b	78. b	79. b	80. b
81. b	82. b	83. a	84. b	85. a	86. b	87. b	88. a	89. b	90. a
91. b	92. a	93. a	94. b	95. b	96. a	97. a	98. a	99. b	100. a
101. a	102. b	103. a	104. a	105. b					

ANSWER KEY

Chapter 4

1. b	2. b	3. a	4. b	5. a	6. a	7. b	8. b	9. a	10. b
11. a	12. a	13. a	14. b	15. a	16. b	17. a	18. b	19. a	20. b
21. b	22. a	23. a	24. a	25. b	26. a	27. a	28. a	29. a	30. a
31. a	32. b	33. b	34. b	35. a	36. b	37. b	38. b	39. b	40. a
41. a	42. b	43. b	44. b	45. b	46. b	47. a	48. a	49. b	50. b
51. a	52. a	53. b	54. a	55. a	56. b	57. a	58. a	59. a	60. b
61. b	62. a	63. a	64. b	65. a	66. b	67. a	68. b	69. b	70. b
71. b	72. b	73. b	74. a	75. b	76. a	77. a	78. b	79. b	80. a
81. b	82. a	83. a	84. a	85. a	86. b	87. a	88. a	89. b	90. a
91. b	92. a	93. a	94. b	95. a	96. b	97. b	98. a	99. a	100. b
101. b	102. b	103. b	104. a						

Chapter 5

1. a	2. a	3. b	4. b	5. b	6. a	7. a	8. a	9. b	10. a
11. a	12. a	13. a	14. a	15. b	16. b	17. b	18. a	19. b	20. a
21. a	22. b	23. b	24. b	25. b	26. a	27. b	28. a	29. b	30. a
31. b	32. b	33. b	34. a	35. a	36. a	37. a	38. a	39. b	40. a
41. a	42. b	43. a	44. a	45. b	46. b	47. a	48. a	49. a	50. b
51. b	52. a	53. b	54. b	55. a	56. a	57. b	58. a	59. a	60. a
61. a	62. b	63. b	64. b	65. a	66. a	67. a	68. a	69. b	70. a
71. b	72. b	73. a	74. b	75. a	76. a	77. b	78. a	79. b	80. a
81. b	82. a	83. a	84. a	85. b	86. a	87. a	88. a	89. b	90. b
91. a	92. b	93. b	94. b	95. a	96. a				

Chapter 6

1. b	2. a	3. b	4. a	5. a	6. b	7. a	8. b	9. a	10. a
11. a	12. a	13. b	14. a	15. b	16. b	17. a	18. b	19. b	20. b
21. b	22. a	23. a	24. b	25. a	26. b	27. b	28. b	29. a	30. a
31. a	32. a	33. a	34. b	35. b	36. b	37. b	38. a	39. a	40. b
41. a	42. a	43. b	44. b	45. a	46. b	47. b	48. b	49. b	50. b
51. a	52. a	53. a	54. a	55. a	56. b	57. a	58. b	59. a	60. b
61. a	62. b	63. b	64. a	65. b	66. b	67. a	68. a	69. a	70. b
71. a	72. b	73. b	74. a	75. b	76. b	77. b	78. b	79. a	80. b
81. b	82. a	83. a	84. a	85. b	86. b	87. b	88. a	89. a	90. b
91. a	92. b	93. b	94. a	95. b	96. b	97. a	98. b	99. a	100. a
101. a	102. a	103. b	104. a	105. b	106. b	107. b	108. b	109. a	110. a
111. a									

Chapter 7

1. b	2. a	3. b	4. a	5. b	6. b	7. a	8. a	9. a	10. b
11. a	12. b	13. a	14. a	15. a	16. a	17. a	18. b	19. a	20. b
21. a	22. a	23. a	24. a	25. b	26. a	27. b	28. b	29. a	30. a
31. b	32. a	33. a	34. b	35. a	36. a	37. a	38. b	39. b	40. b
41. b	42. a	43. a	44. a	45. b	46. b	47. b	48. b	49. b	50. a
51. b	52. b	53. b	54. b	55. b	56. b	57. a	58. b	59. a	60. a
61. b	62. a	63. a	64. a	65. b	66. a	67. b	68. b	69. a	70. b
71. a	72. b	73. b	74. b	75. a	76. b	77. a	78. b		

Chapter 8

1. a	2. b	3. b	4. b	5. a	6. b	7. b	8. a	9. b	10. b
11. b	12. b	13. b	14. a	15. a	16. b	17. a	18. a	19. a	20. b
21. a	22. b	23. a	24. b	25. b	26. b	27. b	28. a	29. b	30. a
31. a	32. a	33. b	34. a	35. a	36. a	37. b	38. b	39. a	40. b
41. a	42. b	43. a	44. a	45. b	46. a	47. a	48. b	49. a	50. b
51. b	52. b	53. a	54. a	55. b	56. b	57. a	58. a	59. a	60. b
61. a	62. a	63. a	64. a	65. b	66. b	67. b	68. a	69. b	70. a
71. a	72. a	73. a	74. b	75. a	76. b	77. a	78. b	79. a	80. b
81. b	82. a	83. a	84. b	85. b	86. a	87. b	88. b	89. a	90. b
91. b	92. b	93. a	94. b	95. b	96. a	97. b	98. a	99. a	100. b
101. b	102. b	103. a	104. a	105. b					

Chapter 9

1. b	2. b	3. a	4. b	5. a	6. b	7. b	8. b	9. b	10. b
11. b	12. a	13. a	14. b	15. b	16. b	17. a	18. a	19. a	20. a
21. b	22. b	23. a	24. a	25. b	26. a	27. a	28. a	29. b	30. a
31. a	32. b	33. b	34. b	35. a	36. b	37. a	38. b	39. a	40. a
41. b	42. a	43. a	44. a	45. a	46. a	47. a	48. a	49. a	50. a
51. a	52. a	53. a	54. a	55. a	56. a	57. a	58. b	59. a	60. a
61. b	62. a	63. b	64. a	65. b	66. a	67. b	68. a	69. b	70. b
71. b	72. a	73. a	74. a	75. a	76. a	77. a	78. b	79. a	80. a
81. a	82. a	83. a	84. b	85. a	86. b	87. a	88. b	89. b	90. b
91. b	92. a	93. b	94. b	95. a	96. a	97. a	98. a	99. a	100. b
101. b	102. a	103. a	104. a	105. b	106. a	107. a	108. b	109. b	110. a
111. b	112. b	113. b	114. a						

Chapter 10

1. b	2. b	3. b	4. b	5. b	6. a	7. a	8. b	9. b	10. a
11. b	12. b	13. b	14. a	15. b	16. b	17. b	18. a		

www.ingramcontent.com/pod-product-compliance
Lightning Source LLC
Chambersburg PA
CBHW082051230426
43670CB00016B/2853